Memories
Of
Lockdown

2nd book of the trilogy

First published in the United Kingdom in 2023 by
The Choir Press

ISBN: 978-1-78963-352-8

Cover design by Bob Hellyer
www.BobHellyer.art
Typeset by Phoenix Media
www.phoenixmediadesign.com

Thanks Mum & Dad
for your inspiration

Thank you for the Rose

"Thank you to my wonderful family and friends -
without all of you there would be no book"

Introduction

One year on… I hope you will enjoy reading continuing stories from some of my Book One writers and new stories from writers who have just joined us for Book Two. I think it's a lovely combination and hope you will agree.

When I started working on Book One of the Trilogy in June 2021 and told my friends and family that my aim was to publish before Christmas, I was greeted by some disbelieving comments, but there it was. The timing was very important to me - I was thrilled!

Book One was being read in many countries across the world by the New Year of 2022 and to say I was very pleased would be an understatement. I received some lovely comments and reviews.

Sadly there is still suffering across the world and there is still a great divide between people with their different views and opinions, but I continue to believe that reading each other's stories will help us understand that we each have our own Truth and the world will be a better place when we understand and respect each other more. The importance of speaking our Truth without the ego of 'having to be right.'

Dropping into our hearts to know our Truth and agreeing without judgement that "We don't all see things the same way."

Enjoy

'It's All About The Children'

Rosanne

Well - what a year - looking back it seems to have flown by and yet so much has happened.

My story continues from precisely where I left it, meeting each day with optimism and joy and making sure each day is a good one.

The winter of 2021/2022 came and went unremarkably. I hadn't planned on being unwell and so it threw my rhythm and I had to surrender. Once again I found myself in an unexpected circumstance which I accepted as another 'gift of time' and although it was frustrating and at times a bit scary… looking back, I used my time well and learnt a lot. I continued on my journey of reflection and patience, intermingled with grieving for all that had gone.

I had become unwell suddenly during the second week of December and a doctor sent me off to hospital for tests. Within hours of my arrival at the hospital, one of the doctors announced that I did not have the acute diagnosis I had been sent in for and instead I had covid and would be transferred to a covid ward. That was definitely not on my Christmas wish list! Having checked that I could discharge myself at any time and being assured that I could, I allowed myself to be wheeled off into the never ending corridors and lifts through the hospital and, for a reason I'll never know, I was wheeled into a private room and not a ward.

Within half an hour of being in my room a nurse arrived asking me if I would like to take experimental covid drugs while I was in hospital. I declined. I also decided not to take the steroids that were prescribed as I felt the covid diagnosis was not accurate; I brought them home as a souvenir!

Kind, gentle nurses came and went - they were quiet and did their jobs with such care, they were like angels. A consultant came to see me and we had a long discussion about what would happen in the year to come and after 2 days of reassuring everyone who looked after me that, in my opinion, they would all get back to visit their home countries during the next year, it was time to go home. I had immediately felt better on arrival in hospital having had a drip for a few hours - it had cured my nausea and being able to eat and drink again I knew I could recover. Blood tests had consistently been clear and I was officially discharged. Although I allegedly had covid, no one checked on my home circumstances, quarantine etc. All very odd.

Good to be home and the long haul to recovery started. I took homeopathic remedies and little by little I gained some energy and by the end of February I was out walking the dogs again, though I still had a way to go.

A succession of life-changing events had followed one after the other in a relatively short space of time over the past few years, and I had done what people do - 'just kept going'. However, in reality the toll of each event has to be faced and dealt with otherwise it is always lurking as 'unfinished business' in the background which is no good at all…

People who had always been in my life had gone in death or by choice, the forever family home in England and my own family home and life in Spain gone - so many changes to process and alongside all the personal change, the world was changing before my eyes.

There was sadness and grief to work through but, as in a beautiful metamorphosis, over time I began to realise how liberating and empowering it felt and how wonderful it was to have the opportunity of choice.

All my life I have followed my heart and all my life I have been happy with where it has led me - I wouldn't change a thing! It was, and is my essence, and I have never been more grateful for anything!

Let's leap forward into spring - the hope it brings is always joyous and the spring of 2022 was no different, in fact I felt it was the welcoming in of a very significant year. Many were focussing on getting back to some resemblance of normality, many had put off travelling for a couple of years and were now keen to get on a flight somewhere. The constant talk of the virus lessened while the continuing talk of climate change got louder and then talk of war in Europe, until one morning we woke to find the covid headlines replaced with war in the Ukraine.

Spring brought a move. I moved into a new house which instantly felt like home, in fact it felt like I had lived there or in a very similar house before. I loved it and settled in immediately. Peaceful and calm with all that I needed and the icing on the cake was my small walled courtyard garden; for the first time in my life I

became a bit of a gardener and loved it!

With the early summer came a change of energy for me which led to meeting new friends and discovering new passions and projects - what a happy time! Having returned to England from Spain

during the first lockdown in 2020 I had not had the chance to meet people as you would normally for many reasons, and partly by choice. Now 2 years on I was discovering beautiful new friendships and the timing was perfect.

I have always believed 'everything happens for a reason and in perfect time' and have reminded myself of this daily, sometimes more than once in a day, over the past years.

The summer of 2022 in England was full of sunshine and that's exactly how I felt.

I have become involved in two new health related projects - both excited me enormously the minute I heard of them, the thought of offering people health care based on informed choice and not purely on the big business of pharmaceutical drugs and financial gain was like music to my ears, and I have thought for a long time that 'energy healing' is part of our exciting way forward in the world of health. Of course it's not new, it's just new and becoming available to many of us - until now it has only been available to those that could afford it. My future and the future of those around me includes a health system or systems available to everyone, where everyone is heard and seen and where everyone can make their own informed decisions and receive the treatment they choose.

Mum and Dad always gave me such good advice and the last thing Dad said to me was "It's time for you to go and be happy." This was in the last couple of months of his life; he looked at me, smiling and in that instant his eyes were bright.

I believe at that moment we both knew that this was our time to let go, let go of each other in this lifetime. It was time for Dad to let go of his wish for me to take him home, in the realisation that his home, his next beautiful destination was with Mum. I finally said goodbye to him some weeks later when he was far along his transition, or perhaps already with her. I look forward to being with you both again, but not yet as I have much to do.

Thank you Mum and Dad, our ancestors too, for walking beside me at this time of evolution, of endings and new beginnings, for giving me your trust and strength for which I have so much daily gratitude. Thanks to you all I walk without fear.

I have taken Dad's advice and know that he and Mum are smiling as they see how happy I am and how much happier I will be in my future. "It's all exactly as it's meant to be and I will always live in wonderment and love ... forever optimistic."

LOVE

"Follow your Heart
Let the Light Lead Through the Darkness
Back to a Place you Once Knew..."

Jan

Happy and a little tipsy at the Ritz in London

And just like that, it's 2022. Time, literally it seems, has flown by.

So, what happened to me and my family…

August 2020 – No travel allowed in or out from Western Australia. After my mum's health issues, I returned to WA and prayed constantly that mum continued to gain her strength, learn how to accept, and live with her bucket of medications and adapt to a new life. A life a little less hectic, a little less cheese and a lot less gin. None of these topics were an easy fix, but she took it on board and was grateful that she had fought hard and won, but needed to make some changes to make sure her heart could still be strong. She listens to her body and does what she must to stay well, fit and active – pretty good for an 86 year old.

Looking back over these 2 years or so, it seems as if we have all in some way gained some positives of the time we have spent in lockdown, with or without our friends and family. We spent more time in the very place we pay for all our lives - our homes. We seem to have very organised cupboards and we read those books we always wanted to, painted those walls and had some valuable time back – very strange.

Forward to May 2022.

I have just returned from a 5 week trip back to the UK and this time it was an utter joy to travel. Western Australia had lifted all the travel restrictions; however, masks were still mandatory in the airports and on board the flight. Keeping your eye on the prize of being back with friends and family means all those issues are no effort and a very, very small price to pay, to hug and hold once again those people you cherish most in life.

We spent our time having family days out, weekends in London, High Tea at The Ritz, Spa Days with girlfriends, 60th's, 80th's and a wedding in Devon in the sunshine. My mum is doing really well and has booked her flight down to Western Australia to be with me for my birthday in December.

My story ends well and I know that others have lost loved ones and suffered immeasurably, so I don't take anything lightly. I am very happy to have my freedom again and move around whenever I want to. I have not yet had Covid, despite all the miles I have travelled and all the people I have mixed with – maybe I am lucky and long may that be the case!

Peter English

My Lockdown Memories

We knew it was coming, we'd been following the news about the virus emerging from Wuhan, China via Milan in Italy. Little did we know that it was about to turn into a two-year hiatus!

As the news unfolded, we left on 8th March 2020 for a four day skiing trip up in Arinsal, Andorra, a six-and-a-half-hour drive north from Javea, Alicante Spain were we live.

At the time, I was the Social Secretary of our local sailing club when the Spanish government started announcing the beginning of lockdown for the following week. None of us really knew what this meant, or what the implications were going to be. From our hotel room, I wrote an email to the committee on 10th March to suggest cancelling or postponing various social and sailing events planned for the near future. My request was challenged by the Chairman and Vice-Chairman, their feeling was that it wasn't nearly bad enough yet to be cancelling things.

We left Andorra for home on 12th and the very next day, lockdown came into full force across Spain, we only just made it back in time because one of the rules was no travel between regions, you couldn't travel to another province or community, like a county. Needless to say, a few days later, the club cancelled all sailing and social events for the foreseeable future.

Lockdown in Spain, at least in our Valencian Community meant what it said – lockdown! We couldn't believe the news from England where lockdown seemed to be a bit of a joke. On TV, we saw gatherings in parks and on beaches, they showed the extremely lenient attitude of the police politely asking people not to gather in groups but without enforcing any strict regime or punishment for disobeying rules. Of course, the UK enjoyed amazing weather at that time, week after week of sunshine and warmth, how could people resist not going out to parks and beaches? In Spain, it was the opposite, the weather was atrocious - cold, wet, windy and wintery conditions which lasted for six weeks in March and April. It couldn't have been worse, being cooped up, barely allowed to go out anywhere, apart from gardening we couldn't even take advantage of our garden, we stayed in with the heating on, right through April.

There are two types of police here in Spain, the local police who deal with day to day living and petty crimes, and then there are The Guardia who are as close to military as you can get. They wear full combat gear, carry machine guns and look intimidating. You don't mess with The Guardia. Our lockdown was strict; there were armoured military vehicles parading the beaches, there were reports of people facing hefty fines of between 2000 and 5000 Euros if caught being 'out' or being on the beach or paddling.

With bars, restaurants and most shops closed, it was pretty grim and characterless, considering the place is normally buzzing with activity. Naturally, apart from food, or potential lack of it, I was concerned about my dwindling beer supply. Only one person at any one time was allowed to go in a car to go shopping, you had to have a written shopping list or a receipt, you were not allowed to just go and get a few items, it had to be a substantial supply. If you didn't comply with these rules and were caught, you faced being prosecuted and they were stopping people, so people obeyed and followed the rules! I obliged of course and little by little, the beer stock started to build up nicely.

They warned us that a vaccination programme would become mandatory, that there would be checks and later – we didn't know it at the time – vaccination passports that would become compulsory in order to travel. I didn't believe it would happen, or maybe I didn't want to believe it. I didn't think they would be able to vaccinate everybody.

There was this huge fear issue, portrayed by the media but it really got to people. One example, we have friends in our sailing club who felt vulnerable and would not sail with people who were unvaccinated. Is this what it was coming down to, segregation amongst friends? Oh they had their reasons but you believe what you believe, whether you agree or not with the whole vaccination issue but it is sad that this virus was forcing people apart. It's not for me to dictate whether people should be vaccinated or not, it's up to each and every individual to make their choice, informed or otherwise. I know so many people who got vaccinated because they wanted to travel, they felt they wouldn't be able to travel unless vaccinated. Personally, I think that's for the wrong reason.

We watched in horror the daily number of reported deaths, the statistics, the warnings, the restrictions and with this complete lockdown, began to question what is actually going on here? What is this really about? Is this just a pandemic or is there more we don't know about?

Then there were the masks, the compulsory wearing of them, sanitisers and plastic gloves in shops and supermarkets. We saw people driving alone in a car wearing a mask; that's no different from a man going to bed alone wearing a condom, just in case! Were people using them to protect themselves or out of respect for others? Did people not realise that the wearing of gloves in a store does little or nothing to protect you or them, they still touch things, themselves, products so it makes no difference whether it's a bit of plastic glove or their skin unless they change the glove every time they touch something! If this virus is so contagious and deadly, how can it be stopped by a mask and plastic gloves? There were many flaws in the overall system for my liking. I began to question it more and more.

We watched the sensational British TV news which was dominated by Covid statistics every news bulletin. It became increasingly tedious and boring, we began to wonder where it was all leading to. The first panic of course was about ventilators, they thought that was the answer to save the world. Certain companies were awarded massive contracts for making them along with PPI equipment. Jobs for the boys! We couldn't believe what we were seeing.

Here in Spain there were stories of overwhelming numbers of elderly sick people dying in large numbers in care homes because there wasn't the manpower to help them. It could have been easy to get depressed but one thing that raised our spirits was the determination and camaraderie amongst neighbours with the two-minute daily ritual at 8pm of everyone chanting, banging or clapping outside, not just once a week as in England. We went on our balcony to join in and share the moment each evening religiously. People we'd never met before were waving and shouting at us so we did the same back which sent tingles down my spine and created an amazing atmosphere. We always said we'd go across to those people behind us when it was over but to our delight, they beat us to it and a lovely Spanish man came to introduce himself one evening and offered to cook us a paella at his place. Mind you, that was a year and a half ago and he hasn't been back with the invitation so I think we need another pandemic to rally people together just so that we can go to his place for dinner!

Travel and tourism suffered greatly with the closure of airports, flights cancelled, restaurants and bars were closed, non-essential shops were closed. I recall only supermarkets, garages and chemists remained open. Not only did it affect incoming tourism to Spain, it also meant that we couldn't go anywhere either, not only abroad but even for a break here in Spain somewhere. PCR and Antigen tests were not yet available, I don't think they had even been invented then.

There are always plenty of jobs to do living in a villa with a large garden and pool - repairs, painting, gardening etc but all the shops and builders merchants were closed making it impossible to obtain materials. I became adept at 'dumpster-diving' as Tanya my Canadian wife likes to call it. The system here for disposing of rubbish is to take it yourself to the

bins area where there is a recycling system. It's amazing what people throw out and what you can find and in these desperate times, I found all sorts of useful things. At one time I found two overhead lights, each with two bulbs, the sort you find over a mirror in a bathroom. I fitted them in my store room which didn't even have any electricity so during the lockdown, I wired it from a room next door, found a switch, cable, conduit and the two lights – all at the dump! I was so pleased with myself. Gradually as, lockdown eased, we could order things online from builders merchants and then go to the store to collect, long before they opened up fully. My wife had given me a beer making kit for Christmas, this was the perfect time to get practicing, so I did and produced my first brew during lockdown. I had loads of bottles, a big plastic tub, a hydrometer, the hops and malt kit. All I needed was water, some sterilising, lots of patience and a bit of time, which I had lots of. A couple of weeks later, my concern over beer shortages was over, I was swimming in it.

Our pool needed re-grouting, a job I probably wouldn't have undertaken on my own but the thing to emphasise is that I had time, lots of it so I managed to buy the grout online and then all I had to do was empty the pool, clean and re-grout then fill it. I say 'all I had to do', it was actually a massive job plus 350 Euros worth of water to refill it.

I suppose these were a few of the positive things about lockdown. We were never bored, there were plenty of things for us to do as long as we could get materials and supplies. On the negative side was a complete and sudden stop to our little business and consequently - income. We were involved with holiday lettings and rented our own apartment downstairs plus a couple of other properties we helped to let for the owners. Of course, with Covid restrictions, no one was allowed to travel, they weren't booking or even enquiring. Luckily, we didn't reply on the UK market, the

Brits were no longer coming, nor were the French or Dutch but eventually Spanish clients came, from Madrid, Valencia or the north of Spain. We made the best of it under the circumstances, the camaraderie was strong; one of our neighbours put up a huge sign painted on a sheet across their front gate saying: 'Sigue sonrisa – Keep smiling'. Little things like that plus the daily chanting kept us going. We persevered through the summer, we didn't have a complete end to a first lockdown like in England, it eased but didn't end here in Spain, it just went on and on and then in October, we saw that the second lockdown had been announced in England.

With no end in sight, we decided to try and book a three-day break in January 2021 somewhere here in Spain. We were not allowed to travel out of the Valencian province and browsing online, we found an inn in a little town called Ademuz, right up in the top corner of Valencia bordering onto Castille y La Mancha, the next province. We had to choose a place that offered meals as restaurants were still closed, hence the inn. It was a fantastic break with excellent hospitality and meals with drinks all included, just what we needed after having been restricted for so long. At dinner on the first evening, we were asked what we would like to drink, I said I'd like a beer and my wife wanted some white wine. We expected a glass of each. The proprietor came back after a few minutes. Bang! Goes a whole litre bottle of beer, Bang! as a bottle of white wine was put on the table. Halfway through the meal I asked for some red wine. Bang! A whole bottle on the table. I thought this is going to cost us dearly but the same thing happened the second evening and there was no extra charge for these drinks, it was all included. Such generous hospitality I do relish indeed! The way up to Ademuz follows a route, which for some 10 kilometres leaves the border of Valencia, crosses into the next province Castille y La Mancha and later re-enters Valencia. The road ends in Ademuz and you have to take that road as it's the only one to get there, but on the return journey, we were stopped by La Guardia on the provincial border, asking us where we were going. "Javea" I said. Then he asked me to show my residency card which has my address on. He waved me on but the joke of this was that I was stopped for crossing provinces, yet there is no other option. What were they doing there checking people? I have no idea, just doing their job I suppose!

Two and a half years on, there is still an uneasy feeling as if the virus could start up again, with another strain or mutation into something different. How much of this is fear? Now we have monkeypox, whatever next? And after that? It goes on and on. The human body is designed to resist infection and is a self-healing mechanism but we have lost the ability to live close to the earth and modern medicine is what we have become used to. This explains why people have so much faith in their doctor and modern medical practices.

In summing up, I do question what we've learned from all of this. We still don't know where this virus originated, we're told many different things, some theories have been de-bunked, by whom and why, I have no idea! I strongly believe we're not told everything, there are definitely cover-ups, lots of corruption and huge amounts of money changing hands.

I mentioned theories above, so whilst pontificating, let me get this off my chest about conspiracy theories because there are many accusations flying around and they tend to put people into categories. If there is the faintest, remotest, tiniest little chance that something could be true, then it can neither be a conspiracy nor a theory - and can it be proven it's not true?

In most cases, no it can't.

I was once told that intelligence is measured by the ability to question things, as a scholar might in his or her studies. It's not measured by the number of qualifications you might have, degrees or examination results. Those are merely testing the power of recall under time constraints, that's not proper intelligence. Are people who question things more intelligent? Maybe. The alternative is to fall into the category of the do-gooders who conform to everything, believe everything they're told and have total faith in the system.

Those who know me will know which side of the fence I'm on, the rest of you can judge for yourself. No, the earth is not flat - but it did have a moment's respite, a brief chance to breathe and regenerate, albeit momentarily.

Janet Jackson Tyler Lummer

Since my last letter to you all, I have travelled from:
Spain to Italy, back to Spain. Spain to Germany, back to Spain.
Spain to Germany, to America. Back to Germany, back to Spain.

Pandemic travels are MTAN (more than a notion). The paperwork to travel now is exhausting. It has taken the joy out of travelling for me. Once I get to where I am going and am in the house, then I am ok, but the actual process of buying tickets and getting QR codes for the different countries is crazy complicated. At times the information I received had not been updated which created confusion. Rules and regulations were changing every 2 weeks, or from day to day. One country told me one thing, and then I got to the other country and they would tell me another - "Oh no we do not do that anymore." "But THEY said I could do that" … "Sorry it has changed"… Sometimes I did not know if I was coming or going. On one trip I had to cry and start shaking before someone would help me get what I needed to be able to board the plane. The ticket person said "It is too bad the rules changed and you should have checked, we cannot help you" but an information person saw how upset I was and she helped me (even though she was not suppose to) and I will ALWAYS be grateful for her loving heart (Ryanair information desk). God kept me healthy through all my travels. I was flying through the holiday season. Thanksgiving and Christmas and New Year.

After the crazy and lovely holidays I was due for my booster in January. I was notified 3 times, but because I am not a SMS reading person I did not see the notices, so I missed my appointment. However, they did not give up and sent me another appointment that I did see, and I went. That was one of the nicest experiences I have ever had at a hospital anywhere in the world. My appointment was at the general hospital in Alicante, Spain. It was a large white tent that had been constructed for the times when there were so many Covid patients, that they had to add on space for more people to be treated. Now they are used for administering vaccines. It was a bright sunny day and when I arrived I was the only person in the reception room. There had to have been at least 15 doctors and nurses at my disposal, plus clerks to take my information. ALL with a smile and a kind word to say. I was blown away by the actual love I felt in the room.

I was asking a lot of questions like:
Why can I not have Pfizer since my other shots were Pfizer?
Did you run out of Pfizer?

In Germany I had a friend receive Pfizer 3 times because she was told it is better to get the same one, but in other countries people are told it is better to mix them with a different one (I received Moderna) so why was it different? They said politely they did not know, but in Spain they mix them. My thought was they just ran out of Pfizer so the used Moderna because they are both the vaccines that do not have a live virus in them. So, with all my questions they could see I was nervous about having to mix my shots!!!! The clerk walked me over to the doctor and told her my name. The doctor  HUGGED me and said "Janet, everything will be alright, come in and sit right here" in such a sweet and endearing manner. The shot was perfectly executed and I went home feeling great and I was only sleepy for the rest of the day, and the next day I was feeling normal. I truly believe it was easy on my body because I was treated with such care. Again love conquers ALL.

BUT I do not want to hear about having to take a 4th shot of ANYTHING. I am finished now with this shot business. If 3 are not enough and you have not figured it out by now, you will have to come to my house and get me, because I am not interested in taking one more shot for the same thing again. If 3 shots do not keep me out of the hospital nothing else will!!!!! I am sure we are going to have to repeat this process once a year (hopefully 1 shot only) and that is all I am willing to take. I need to travel in different parts of the world to help other people so taking 1 shot a year to keep others and myself healthy, I will comply.

My son and I have stayed healthy throughout the pandemic and we are so grateful for all that have prayed for us and all the blessings that God has bestowed on us which gives us Peace.

Always In Spirit.
Janet Jackson Tyler Lummer

Lola Angelina

I live in a small village in the region of Alicante in Spain. I'm 16 years old and I'm about to start my first year of Baccalaureate.

My story starts on Thursday 12 March 2020. We were in La Molina, Spain. It was the last night of our ski trip, we would return home the next day after our last ski lesson. We were aware that COVID-19 was going around and it was supposedly affecting a lot of people, but we didn't think it would leave China. Still, knowing this, we decided to go on the trip, what was the worst that could happen? Little did we know, our lives as we knew them were about to change drastically. As I was saying, that Thursday was the last night of our little holiday and we wanted to have a great time.

I will always remember the moment when a friend came and

told us that there would be no classes for two weeks because of COVID-19. "Don't talk nonsense, it's not going to happen," we told him, but how wrong we were. He told us it had been in the news, but we thought he was exaggerating. Well, there was some hope, we would do anything not to go to school. We didn't want to get excited just in case. I remember that my mum called me that same night and told me that the supermarkets were short of products and that there was no more toilet paper. "Why was everyone so desperately buying toilet paper?" I asked myself. I still don't know the answer to my question. I don't think anyone knows, but since it was something everyone else was doing, everyone went along with it. Follow the herd. The only thing I remember is thinking that the world had gone mad and panicked for no reason.

The next morning, Friday 13th, we woke up and were told that we had to immediately pack up and go home. We were all a bit confused as to what was going on. We didn't want to go home as we still had a long day of skiing and fun ahead of us. We were told that if we didn't leave then and there, we would stay stuck at the hotel and we wouldn't be able to go home. The teachers seemed calm, they didn't make a big deal out of it but some of the students were really scared. I remember that while we were waiting for the bus, some men wearing masks and gloves came in to set up hydroalcoholic gel and mask machines. What I didn't know at the time was that it would be my last day away from home for many months. As my friend had said, classes were cancelled, but not only for two weeks, we didn't return to school for the rest of the school year.

Us students had all our books in our lockers, and as we needed them to do the homework we were assigned by our teachers, we were allowed to go to school to collect our things. The building was different, there were arrows everywhere showing you which way to walk and little roundabouts that you had to go around to keep order. At first, when I saw this I thought it was some kind of joke, but when I got told off for going the "wrong way" I realised they were very serious about it. We looked like robots and I really didn't like it. After all, I guess it really is about control.

Days were eternal, I had so much work to hand in and I was struggling to keep up. The teachers must have thought we were machines, because the amount of homework they sent us was unbelievable.

I live in a flat, so the only source of fresh air I have is a small balcony. I love the beach, and because I lived shut in my house, it was horrible not to be able to go out and sunbathe and swim. The beach is my special place and I've loved it ever since I was little. This one particular day it was pouring with rain, but after months of being locked at home, I couldn't stand being in my room all day, so I took the huge amount of schoolwork I had, put on a coat and sat on the balcony. I felt like I was going crazy and I needed to get out. It was like this every day until June, when I was finally able to leave the house. The first thing I did was go for a walk in the countryside with my friend and her dog. It was like a weight was lifted off my shoulders, and I was finally happy again, even though I knew it wasn't over yet.

Summer finally arrived and I spent my whole time at the beach as I had been looking forward to. I was happy. Well, as happy as I could be, because shortly after, the people I thought of as my friends started leaving me aside. At first I didn't understand why, but I then realised it was because we had different opinions and beliefs over Covid, which didn't bother me at all, but they thought differently. I guess this is the risk you take when you speak your mind.

After three months of summer holiday I went back to school. We had to wear masks all day and it was suffocating. One day the vice director of my school pulled me out of class and threatened to suspend me if I didn't wear my mask properly. She told me "Do you want to be remembered as the girl who never wore her mask and as a result harmed everyone and made people die from this disease?" I gave her a simple answer "Yes". She wasn't expecting that answer and she looked rather shocked. Those words stuck in my head. It's such a manipulative thing to say. It affected me at first, everyone had seen me get called out of class and they were all asking what had happened. I was angry and quite upset over the whole situation, but a few hours later I was completely over it and didn't really care about what she had said.

I didn't understand how a piece of material covering your face is going to protect you. However, I understand that people think differently to me and I respect that. Everyone has different opinions and perspectives.

Anyways, did I start wearing my mask properly? No. I didn't feel threatened by the vice director, if she wanted to suspend me that was fine by me, that way I could get a break from people like her and just stay at home. I always wore my mask under my nose even though I kept getting told to put it on properly.

This brings me to today. Two years after this pandemic started I can say that in tough times you really get to see who really cares about you and loves you. Speaking the truth is the best possible thing you can do. Don't change the way you are or the way you think just because someone tells you to. People may leave your side, but after all, if they do, they aren't really worth it.

Brenda

Second Phase

When we initially entered the first lockdown, it was a little scary, going into an unknown situation, being bombarded with a media frenzy, half expecting the horsemen of the apocalypse to appear. We now know we were told some truths, but mostly the wrong information.

As a psychic medium, I was trying to help people traumatised by fear.

On the positive side, I did feel that people were coming together, helping each other, I was hoping the kindness would last, that we would change our priorities. I now know I was being idealistic.

The vaccine programme was proof of that. As somebody who chose not to take the vaccine, I was shocked by the nasty comments and the number of people who accused me of spreading the virus. Between the vaccine and Brexit, we seem to have created a division and lack of understanding.

We all have free will in our beliefs and decisions and I am still idealistic and hope for more kindness. I feel the last 18 months have been tough, lots of changes and decisions, reassessing relationships, work, family, the whole scenario. Not easy, but necessary.

Let's hope we can be there for each other.

Pattie

Christmas Day 2021: It is 4 months on from my last summary in Rosanne´s great book 'Memories of Lockdown'.

I find myself in Spain spending Christmas Day by myself – definitely not what my intention was. I had thought I would be spending it with my family in the UK, but when I had talked to my son about visiting I was informed that it was the turn of the other grandparents to be there. Naturally I felt very sad about that but as I increasingly know that the Universe has my back, I knew it was happening for a reason. Of course my Christmas was a success and I was able to talk to my grandchildren on Facetime!

In previous years I would spend part of the Christmas holidays with my family and part with friends in the UK. Those friends were taking a different path from me, regarding having jabs, so were reticent about me staying with them. We know this division has been growing as time goes on and sadly many members of families and friends have parted company. The discrimination against those of us who chose not to be jabbed, preferring instead to use the body´s own immune system to protect ourselves from Covid was disgraceful. Flying to other countries was made extremely difficult.

In my beautiful part of Spain, the majority of the people, Spanish and other nationalities, have had at least 2 jabs and recently have been queuing up for the booster. That is their choice but unfortunately I believe that they have been hypnotised by the government propaganda with it's constant fear mongering, as have the people of the UK.

At the beginning of the pandemic while I was in lockdown and I heard about a jab, my first reaction was that it would be a good thing to stop the virus, but obviously a vaccination would take time to be invented and trialled before it was safe. This thought was confirmed by a close friend of mine who had worked in clinical research trials for 20 years and who knows what is involved in the process of developing a new vaccine. We talked about it at great length and we both had concluded (along with clear intuitive insight) that we would not be taking the jab.

In the past few months my mind has been blown away by the fact that the majority of the population here CANNOT see what is going on under their noses. We are being controlled and manipulated by the governmental puppets who are in the hands of the cabal/elites/rich families and are turning the population into compliant slaves. I am very sad for the people and do not blame them for losing their power to powerful hypnotism, it's not their fault. I only wish I was in possession of the trigger words and phrases to snap them out of it. That said, however, I KNOW that many more people are starting to become aware that something is not right and hopefully this will lead some of them into being completely spiritually awakened to the truth.

For many years I have had guidance and comfort from the Angelic Realm. The angels have helped me for years so I chat to them often. In recent years I have also been noticing signs so much more, like my mum´s favourite song or repetitive numbers that guide me on my spiritual journey. I feel so privileged to be one of the volunteers here on earth who are helping others through the Ascension process.

5 July 2022: Many energetic developments have occurred now and we are certainly ascending into the 'Age of Love' as predicted, which has been so joyful for those of us who are awakened and have been waiting for this.

The photonic light has been coming into our planet and upgrading our DNA so that our bodies become crystalline. Consequently people are finding that they cannot tolerate certain food and drink and having to move towards more vegetables, fruit, smoothies etc. It makes me laugh that so many of us red wine drinkers now have to dilute a glass of wine with water to be able to digest it.

I am now able to fly within Spain with certain airlines without being discriminated against for not having the jab. Fortunately the UK turned out to be much more open minded than many other countries, so I was able to fly back over the Easter period to be with my family and have quality time and also to have some special time with good friends.

Sadly some countries like Canada and Australia have been very controlling and the non-jabbed were unable to travel by air. The loss of Human Rights has been diabolical and caused enormous stress, frustration, division and mental illness.

One of the most wonderful pieces of news that has lifted my spirits enormously just recently... I had listened to a Youtube interview between Pam Gregory, astrologist, and Katherine McBean, founder of the PHA - 'People's Health Alliance' in the UK. During the interview she explained that healthcare was being given back to the people as the infamous NHS has unfortunately been collapsing for some time and the British people were not getting proper healthcare.

Communities throughout the UK have been following the PHA blueprint to start up 'hubs' that will provide health support for the people. I was thrilled to hear that 140 hubs have already been established and that other countries are doing the same. I immediately sent the video to a friend who I knew would be as excited as I was, and as she is a lady who takes action, she had added a hub for our area of Spain to the PHA by that afternoon! We are now learning all about how to take it forward with wonderful volunteer doctors and nurses plus all kinds of holistic healers and care givers in this area. This is the future!

26 August 2022: I recently returned from a long trip away to friends and family. During my visit to Ireland I visited several sacred sites where I went through powerful energetic spiritual experiences. One in particular was very emotional and memorable at the Hill of Uisneach, known as the Heart Chakra of Ireland. The tour guide explained about the ancient history of the site and led us to a huge boulder/cat stone which is the resting place of Ériu, the goddess of Ireland. It was here that I was overcome by emotion and was aided by a lovely guy on the tour, to release a lot of the trauma that was experienced by my ancestors. My friend and others in the group also experienced a powerful release and healing. We are all affected in different ways by the past and I was glad to have this special release.

As the Ascension continues, I am definitely happy to be drawn more and more into the 5th dimensional energy. It is just amazing how quickly we are manifesting our thoughts, I laugh with friends about how it won´t be long until we are reading each others minds! We are just about managing to get used to changing timelines but sometimes it is very weird.

I was delighted to see how much my family and friends were enjoying their lives in the UK, going to lots of outside social events because of the long, hot summer they were having.

I strongly believe the more we live in love and enjoyment the stronger are the positive vibrations going into the Universe.

People who are controlled by fear, sadly cannot experience joy. Thankfully, most people are on the road to Ascension as predicted and I am forever grateful for living now, during this incredible time of transformation and for the wonderful future ahead of us.

Aisling Mary Melchizedek

Hi beloved souls.
Here we continue our story…

It is a pleasure being able to write and share my insights with you all over this last year after finishing story one.

I'd like to give thanks to you all for reading and liking the first book and for having taken the best out of it for your personal growth. I too thank everyone for their opinions and shares, I loved reading the different aspects all have brought into it, this is what makes it so interesting.

Neutrality is the most important state we can hold without judgement, even if another writer said something you do not resonate with, these times have occurred for us all to look within our own beliefs and thought patterns and ways we handle difficulties or challenges. If you still get triggered by another's opinion or point of view, and it causes an emotional reaction or response, look within, it is only a mere reflection of your own shadow or unhealed trauma you still carry. Turn the mirror and ask yourself why and what exactly is triggering you. If you allow yourself to be honest, you will learn a lot and begin to discover your subconscious mind - expand in consciousness so you can begin to work on your negative ego mind, and get rid of all that no longer serves us for our Ascension Cycle we are all in right now.

That is what I have done after the lockdowns and wish to share with you all, I took the time to really go within for healing deep seeded traumas and causes that still lay dormant and unattended from childhood. I have come across so many adults that still walk around behaving like children, therefore I thought it important to look within and heal anything I still held within my inner child that was still traumatised.

As I mentioned in the first book, my youngest son was with me at my home in Spain during the first lockdown, then he returned to Switzerland where he lives and so I was alone and could dedicate my free time to that introspection. I was so thankful to be able to do so.

Both my sons have spent time with me this year, visiting a few times, and even they realised the personal development I have gone through and the growth that came because of it.

When my sons were growing up, my youngest son lived alone with me for a couple of years while my eldest son chose to return to Switzerland to study and then run the family hotel.

My youngest son is unvaccinated like myself and during the first lockdown we did a lot of research together. He continues to be very awake and informed knowing what is behind the current agenda.

My eldest son is vaccinated as he thought that was the best option for him at that time. Each time he visited me I spoke to him about the truth behind the vaccines and asked him if he would allow me to do a vax clearing on him energetically in a therapy. He agreed. Yay!!! My heart jumped for joy to receive his permission for that. As mothers, we do not wish our children to go through any harmful events or happenings.

Last month when he and my ex-husband came to visit, I was able to do the vax clearing on them both, since my ex-husband also got the shot. It felt amazing knowing that no longer do they have to suffer any form of side effects from it in the future and have released the poison and all the particles that harm the body and soul. That was a huge most wonderful moment of their visit, to get their permission to clear that shot of their bodies and their DNA. This can be done remotely as well - all I need is the permission from the person wanting it done. You can reach out to me, should you repent having gotten it and notice it affecting you in any way. You can find my details on the 'Memories Of Lockdown' website in the writers section. This is part of my mission to help mankind stay sovereign and free.

Life here in Spain where I live, has begun to change for many. I see this in our patients coming to the dental clinic where I work part time. They speak to me and many now regret having taken the vax. They see a change in the entire world and realise that it isn't right to be constantly bombarded by the media with Covid and vax info. They began to question everything when they started feeling side effects and were called for booster shots. Unfortunately this is what mankind needed to awaken to the Truth. Now men and women will no longer be easily manipulated and less will follow the herd; people have started to stand strong in their own pillar of light and truth.

Life has returned to a quieter pace, although the next point on the agenda is that we are now being asked to believe that we no longer have sufficient food, they will try to limit access to us. This we know is a last card which they are holding onto, as well as the weather manipulations. We just need to hang in there knowing that it will soon be over and these dark plans won't succeed. Stand in your sovereignty always, do your energetic shielding daily, raise your vibrations and stay in the love frequency and in your Sacred Heart, and should there be more lockdowns, do as I did, go inwards and heal yourself.

The easiest way is to remain in our comfort zone and continue with our life as usual, hiding from ourselves, escaping, not wanting to confront the inner world, feelings and emotions, basically our own shadows. Most humans live in the external world and search outside of themselves, giving their power away, believing that only another person can heal them. They are too scared to go within, to look and feel the pains that are there.

We all are very conditioned from birth or even prior to birth and hold so many beliefs, opinions, thought-forms and patterns that we inherit from our family and ancestral lineages. They did their best educating us in the way they thought was right, but all the unhealed trauma carries on to the next generation until one person in the generational line begins to heal deeply within, not just themselves but the entire family lineages going back 7 to 30 generations. It is a mission that the soul decides to take on, to help the lineages, the planet, the universe, the multiverse, the omniverse. Each human, meeting that soul, heals themselves simply by their presence of receiving the unconditional love emitted from the heart of that person. That love is being carried in words, written, and spoken, through sounds in light language and begins to nurture, trigger, help, and heal others around them.

The Universe has given me the chance to do all that in the time of lockdown since I had the time and the desire and willpower for personal introspection. I am very fortunate to work with my soul family and tribe in America and Canada, we do a lot of energy work on a regular basis, encompassing the personal, planetary, universal and omniverse levels, the multidimensionality.

With our work, all our own densities we still hold onto in all our levels and bodies, will come to the surface to be seen, looked at, acknowledged and accepted - we can then let them go. It is very freeing and over time one becomes much more aware of the entire complexity of what we are.

I hope you trust or know that we have all come here to develop our spirit and soul, and especially since 2020 it is a huge time for all mankind, for each woman and man to begin to dig deep within, stop looking outside and truly see the potential you hold, to get rid of the densities within so we can all make that change to the wonderful New Earth we are creating. All you see in the external world is beginning to crumble, all the old structures - financial, government (which is governing our mind), health, pharmaceutical, political and the educational systems are breaking apart.

More and more people are waking up, and the P(l)andemic has only helped that to occur. The ones wanting to keep us enslaved, the dark agenda, have shot the bullet into their own direction and it's hitting them every day. They are seeing that we no longer believe all that the media tells us, that we have begun to question and research for ourselves as more is revealed. All they wanted us to believe is not the truth and in no way or form good for mankind. The people that are part of the dark agenda can get out of the dark and return to the light; they became too veiled and forgot where they come from, they feed off the negative rather then the love. Eventually, if they choose, they can also return to source rather then staying here in this loop of reincarnation. We all get that chance.

I was so fortunate as all this started to happen, to not believe the media as my gut feeling or my Intuition was indicating to me that something was not right. When our amazing inner voice begins to speak to us, we must listen, as it is the wisdom of many lifetimes we carry. It is our inner compass guiding us along in all we do, feel, decide, etc.

We are divine sparks that hold the original organic blueprints with all the accumulated knowledge, free of all distortions, reversals and inorganic information which tries to manipulate us in the external world. Reconnecting back to it will lead us exactly to our mission, purpose, highest timeline, and service to others.

We are all LOVE, we are sovereign, we are joy, we are peace, and we are unity, and we will all unite again to go home together as ONE. That is why it is so important to accept each soul as they are, and not criticise or judge them for being different from you, for having a different outlook on life, as we are all family and will unite. Only then can we create this wonderful New Earth where harmony, compassion, innocence, unconditional love, purity, ease and grace is our daily being.

Let us all start here and now with this and if you find it difficult, reach out to a friend or a family member that can support you, being vulnerable and authentic is what we are meant to be, you will be surprised how much you will show and teach others by being that way.

As you all see, this has been and is my daily recipe for life, and I am very grateful to the times of the lockdown as we were all given the opportunity to go within. It is also beautiful that each person could choose how to approach these days of being locked indoors, it's been a blessing on all levels for all of us, just see the good in it all. If it had not happened, there would not be as many awakened souls out there now, and that is fantastic.

I hope this inspired you to reflect on life a little deeper.

I wish you all an amazing Ascension and we will all see us in the 5D and above, each one at their own pace. Sending you all so much love from my heart to yours, and hope you enjoyed this little share, Aho, Shalom, Namaste, I am, we are, Ubuntu.

With all my love, Aisling Mary Melchizedek

Samantha

I could write for days if I was to explain all my reasons for becoming a mental health nurse so to summarise briefly, I suppose I am driven by an innate desire to connect with people.

I am naturally caring and find it a real honour and a privilege to be able to help people in some of their darkest moments. Pre-pandemic, I had an awareness that the healthcare system has many flaws.

Mental health care has leant towards a bio-medical way of working that I tend not to agree with, however, over the years, I feel we have been moving towards a recovery based way of working whereby talking therapies and social inclusion is more at the forefront. Most importantly I believed that despite the flaws, my colleagues and I tried our best with what we were provided with in order to help people in whatever way that we could.

Over the last 15 years, I have worked primarily in acute psychiatric units. I love the people that I meet and although I have been confronted with much sadness, overall the positives have far outweighed the negatives. I had never considered any other line of work. I loved my job and could never see myself doing anything else. Then the pandemic hit and everything changed.

The first time I heard of Covid, I was in an infection control meeting. The facilitator talked about a virus that was making its way across the world and was expected to have deadly consequences. We were advised to make sure our patients had appropriate Treatment Escalation Plans (TEPs) in place because hospitals were expected to become overwhelmed and we may have to accept the fact that hospital beds will be prioritised for those most likely to overcome the illness. A TEP is basically a document that outlines a patient's treatment plan if they were to become too unwell to advocate for themselves. Whether a person is resuscitated or not would be something recorded on a TEP.

As a mental health nurse of working age adults, I do not deal much with TEPs so I found it alarming that it was felt I needed this information. I came away from that meeting feeling terrified. The first thing I did was call my grandparents and urge them to retreat to their holiday home because I knew that on paper, my dear grandfather would not be prioritised for a bed should he need one.

Very quickly the panic spread. Within weeks of that first meeting we were in lockdown. It all happened so fast, my brain could barely process it. At work we quickly discharged anyone who was felt to be at high risk of becoming unwell with Covid. Only those who would genuinely not survive in the community due to either mental or physical ill health remained. Very quickly we were sat in an almost empty hospital. At that time I felt completely unable to question any of it. The whole world had closed around me. The shops, the gyms and the restaurants. This was serious. The world wouldn't react in this way otherwise surely?

However as I adjusted to the changes, my brain started to pick up on things that just didn't quite sit right with me. I can quite confidently state that I work with some of the calmest people in the world. I once witnessed a consultant being shouted at by a huge and very intimidating male patient. The man towered over the consultant and was screaming, shouting and waving his fists. I was convinced that at any moment, the consultant would turn on his heels and run. Instead the louder and more hostile the man became, the calmer and more softly spoken the consultant became. The consultant matched the aggression with equal levels of peace and after some time, the man stopped shouting.

We are very used to working with high stress situations. It takes a lot to ruffle the feathers of most of my colleagues, therefore I could not compute in my brain that these very same people were now completely out of control with panic and fear. I witnessed colleagues screaming at one another for coming within 2 metres or for a mask dropping under a nose.

The management seemed to be doing little to stem the fear. Instead we had almost daily meetings where loaded scary terminology was used. People were being whipped up into a frenzy and I just had this overwhelming sense that things could not possibly become as bad as people feared they would.

As soon as my brain began questioning, red flags were appearing so frequently I was almost unable to keep up. Finally the dreaded wave of Covid had reached us. A patient I knew of on a neighbouring ward had tested positive for Covid. He had been in psychiatric units since the days of institutions and really he should have been admitted to our older adult ward because he was over the age of 70.

However, because he had a non organic mental illness (not a dementia) and was so well known to adult services, he was always admitted to working age wards. I do not know how this man has lived to the age he has considering he has been pumped full of old school anti-psychotics and lives on a diet of pipe tobacco and coffee. I said my prayers for him because I was certain he would not survive, but to my astonishment, he did indeed survive. He required no treatment at all and I was told he puffed his pipe all the way through his Covid experience.

Covid spread to other patients. None of them became unwell with it, however I noticed more alarming words being used such as 'that ward is RIFE with Covid'. What was even stranger for me was that each and every staff member who had come into contact with these patients was sent home and told to stay there for the next ten days. I was told stories about physically well but angry and bewildered staff members being sent home from shifts in droves.

Next we were all encouraged to set up 'track and trace' on our phones. My alarm bells were ringing hard by this point and I refused to follow this procedure. Again I had this sense that I needed to stop myself getting on this fast moving train of panic.
There would be days that I would arrive to work and have half the usual amount of staff because someone had got 'pinged' as being in contact with a Covid case whilst picking up a takeaway dinner the night before. The whole system was a nightmare and I began to make the correlation between the stories of overwhelmed hospitals and how actually this may be associated with the rules around testing and self-isolating.

Unusually for my age and the era I live in, I have never used social media. I began to feel very isolated in my views and thoughts. If I publicly challenged any of the things that didn't make sense, I was made to feel selfish. People would say "Haven't you seen any of the pictures of the nurses with mask marks on their faces after a 12 hour shift?" or "you're a mental health nurse - the general hospitals are overwhelmed". I began to try and find out more from other sources. A friend of mine was a ward sister in a local general hospital. She told me she didn't know how many Covid cases were there when I asked because she was on two weeks annual leave. Annual leave... I thought that was all being cancelled? I contacted friends and relatives who lived in big cities. So far I knew no one who had been unwell with Covid.

Could it be my geographical location? Were the bodies piling up high on the streets of London? No it seems they weren't; my city friends didn't know anyone who had been ill with Covid.

By now I had huge doubts over the quality of the data that was being broadcast to us on a daily basis about Covid hospital admissions. I felt it lacked any form of critical analysis. Maths is my worst subject but even I could see that these numbers being used to terrify us were hugely flawed. I didn't want to know how many people in hospital 'had Covid'. I wanted to know how many people were actually unwell with it. Of all the people on ventilators, I wanted to know how many ventilated patients were ventilated due to Covid alone rather than because they were likely to be ventilated anyway due to other physical co-morbidities.

I began to seriously resent some of the procedures we had in place due to Covid. When anyone was admitted to the ward, they would need a Covid swab and until the results were back they would be kept in the isolation end of the hospital. Well, most complied without an issue and were in and out of the isolation end fairly quickly, however there were some who didn't comply to having a Covid swab, either through personal choice or paranoia. One man was kept in the isolation end for two weeks because he wouldn't accept a swab and this was deemed the 'safe' amount of time to be sure he didn't have Covid. I can tell you that it was worse than prison. He had no outside space or TV (due to wires being a ligature risk). When I raised this as a human rights issue, I was told he could potentially infect our other patients, one of whom was clinically vulnerable to Covid. It was recognised that his conditions were not acceptable, however in these unprecedented times, the risks were weighed up and once again Covid trumped them all.

Over time my spirit was being crushed. 18 months into the pandemic and my ward had not seen one Covid patient. I still didn't know anyone who had been seriously ill with it and my mother who worked in a care home declared it not much different to a normal flu season in terms of mortalities. Yet I was expected on a daily basis to remove people's basic rights and dignities. The rules and procedures were endless. We had begun to see the devastating mental impacts of lockdowns. Where empty hospitals had once stood, we were now bursting at the seams with people who lives had been ruined by lockdowns. Businesses lost, relationship breakdowns, lack of social support and increase in drugs and alcohol use. People were falling apart and so was I. My whole adult life I had worked in a hospital but I could no longer do it. I couldn't inflict these rules upon people when I didn't believe it was in any way proportionate to the risk. I took a new job in an assessment role. I essentially would act as a triage nurse, putting people on the right care pathways and so forth. At the same time as applying for this role, I remember watching the vaccine mandate situation develop within the care home sector.

By this time I had already decided I would not be having the Covid vaccine. There was no way I would be accepting a vaccine made in a rush based on data that I in no way trusted. I was watching with baited breath to see what would happen in the care homes. I was frightened of the vaccine mandate being passed and at that time still very much believed that such an infringement on human rights couldn't occur. I was confident it wouldn't happen. There was no way it could surely?

My mum had been forced to leave her care home job. She had had a stroke and was no longer well enough to do such a physically demanding job. Mum was vaccinated twice by this point; we will never know if there was a link between the stroke and the vaccine.

I would like to point out at this time that I am not a Covid denier. I do think an illness exists, however I have been asked to write an honest account of my story and this is it. I believe the threat was disproportionate to the actual risk. I believe that the very fabric of our society was changed without enough attention to the facts and I believe strongly that this must never happen again.

When the vaccine mandate passed in the care homes and they moved onto the NHS, I knew I had to take action. I was the only unvaccinated person in my team and by now I was used to being constantly questioned and judged for my choices. It only made my resolve stronger and I was finding my voice after all of these months being silenced.

A few key things happened at this time. My aunt came across a group of people with yellow boards picketing about lockdowns. We were introduced to 'Stand In The Park' (SITP) and I can't tell you the enormous relief I felt to realise I had never been alone with my views and concerns. Through this organisation I found out about the app called Telegram and via Telegram I was able to speak with thousands of other NHS staff who were facing losing their jobs. I remember my skin prickling with happiness and excitement the first time I entered a group chat for NHS workers. 'I knew you were all out there somewhere' I typed whilst tears streamed down my cheeks. I was finally able to hear from nurses who had been trained to work on Covid wards but were never needed, also from professionals who were concerned about vaccine damage. In the larger NHS 'fight the mandate' group, I found a colleague who worked in the same Trust as me. Together we formed a smaller sub group on Telegram specifically for our Trust and we set out with a mission to find everyone in our small NHS Trust who was in our position.

Over the next few months my life was under huge strain whilst I fought against the mandate. My marriage was tense, my husband was unvaccinated but more out of laziness than for ethical reasons. He struggled to get on board with why I was so passionate about it. He was scared for our livelihoods, our children and our home however finally and thankfully he could see I wasn't budging and declared he would support me no matter what.

Myself and the other founding member of our group stalked around hospitals at night sticking up posters advertising our group. They were often taken down as quick as they were put up however despite the censorship, steadily over just a couple of months, our group rose in numbers to nearing 150.

We emailed everyone we could think of, had meetings with governors, protested and chipped in money between us to keep individuals in some of the legal cases springing up. Several legal firms were offering to represent NHS staff over the vaccine mandate issue however, it was a costly process for individuals. As a group, we all chipped in a pound each to keep one member of the group in these legal processes.

Our telegram group was buzzing with activity and we fought hard. We fought with every fibre of our beings. Some were already on their way out of the NHS. They no longer wished to stay in a job where they had been treated in such a way. However they still wanted to fight against the vaccine mandate because it went against every principle of informed consent and bodily autonomy that there is.

Work was hell. I remember crying in the office when I was told I shouldn't go on a course because I was about to lose my job. I once came across a patient who had tried taking his own life. His last recorded documentation was from a Doctor who wrote that she had turned him away from the clinic because he was 'unvaccinated and unmasked'. I took the documentation to the highest manager I could and demanded action. I am not confident this was treated with the seriousness it deserved.

Discrimination was open and accepted when it came to the Covid vaccine. I was called at home to be told that when I checked the next rota I would unfortunately not be on it.

The pressure was building and some colleagues buckled and took the vaccine. I can't blame them, the thought had crossed my mind many times. However, I dug deep, ultimately I knew that if I was forced into taking this vaccine against my will then mentally I would be destroyed. The parallels between this and my patients being given medication they did not want when detained was not lost on me. I now began to question everything about my job. I saw how easily a person's views could be treated as delusional because they did not follow what was expected from society. I was now the 'mad one' who wouldn't get vaccinated. If it wasn't for my NHS telegram group and SITP, I would have probably been convinced I'd slipped into a delusional state.

A powerful incident occurred at this time. I went to Glastonbury on a protest and on my way home, stopped to buy a protection crystal because after all, I needed all the help I could get. The next day I was walking my dog and suddenly I had the biggest sense of peace wash over me. I was certain in that moment that everything was going to be OK. I had my health and the people I love and that was all that mattered. No mandate was ever going to take that from me. That sense of peace carried me over the next weeks when finally we heard that we could keep our jobs. How did I feel? Well to be honest I'm still not sure. I would say that I am healing and each day I feel different; angry, sad, disillusioned, confused and hurt but also in the more positive moments I'm proud of myself and know that I've learned a huge amount about the lengths I will go to when I believe in something enough.

As for my future in the NHS, that I do not know. I am grateful that I have been afforded the time to consider my options whilst still having a paying job, however the spark and passion for the job has gone. I've lost faith in many of my colleagues, the organisation and everything I thought it stood for. One thing I do know is that I, with my little crystal from Glastonbury am going to be OK.

Somehow I will use all of this to take me on a new path. One that is more aligned with my spiritual growth and one whereby people's ethical and moral standings are always respected.

Wesley

I have now been working as a Funeral Director for over 3 years and towards the end of summer, beginning of autumn 2021 I noticed to my horror the amount of miscarriages and newborn baby deaths; over 20 in a month in one hospital and a lot of them stored in the adult section due to the baby fridges being full.

It was shocking. I was shocked and with this knowledge I could no longer keep quiet about what I was seeing - I participated in many interviews during October and November. Why was this happening and why wasn't it on the news, pregnant women and young mothers had been persuaded to take the vaccine and they were losing their babies.

It did calm down in the New Year of 2022 but the miscarriages and deaths of babies once again have started to climb over the months and the numbers have now reached a higher number than in 2021.

This year, 2022, has had constant deaths of people dying from issues that haven't been dealt with due to doctors not seeing their patients over the last 2 and a half years. There are also many more sudden deaths in all age groups.

Deaths from suicides before the first lockdown were few and far between. However, in the past 2 years the suicide rate in young men (no women) has risen to one a week and sometimes two; there's nothing more upsetting than seeing a mother saying goodbye to her child.

I hope this doesn't continue into the new phase fast approaching with price increases in food, energy and fuel, or we are in for a rough ride with many more deaths.

Ilona

The first lockdown was a breeze. I was 21 and living with two of my best friends at University in Southampton. We were in our last year, so all our deadlines were pushed back, while many assignments and exams were cancelled. At first we were confused and didn't know what to make of anything. We thought it would just be three weeks to 'flatten the curve' and therefore we immediately decided to have fun.

There was a heatwave, so every morning we blew up a mattress in the garden to sunbathe, made some cocktails, blasted music through a speaker and pretended we were on a girls holiday abroad. We would go on our daily walk around the lake at 6pm as it got cooler, before making dinner and doing some Uni work. This was our daily routine and we loved it! On the first Friday night we had a pizza party. We got dressed up, ordered Dominos, drank wine and did karaoke. It was such a laugh. However, it wasn't long until we realised that this wasn't going to be just 2 weeks.

Suddenly it was a month, then 2 months, then 3… I soon decided that things were being blown out of proportion. I seemed to have a different perspective to my friends. Many of my friends were very paranoid about this virus, probably because their families were all terrified from listening to the news. I made up my own mind, and by looking at the facts I soon realised that the chances of this thing affecting me were non-existent, that the government's decisions on the matter were unreasonable and that the media was exaggerating.

Although my friends didn't share my views at first, we were happy and life was good. I had the best tan I have ever had and felt very peaceful.

The only thing that was troubling me was that I hadn't seen my new boyfriend since March, as he flew back home to Ireland before the lockdown started. However, we spoke every day and our relationship continued to grow (somehow), so by the time he came back to England in June, we felt like we'd known each other forever. We spent the whole of June together without a care in the world, enjoying the sun, sleeping in late, watching films and meeting friends for BBQ's in the park. In June the rest of my friends also came back to Uni (by this point they realised there was nothing to be afraid of) and we tried to live our lives as normal.

Although everything was still closed, we made our own fun, had parties and celebrated our last month at Uni together, ignoring the ridiculous rules. Looking back, it was one of the most enjoyable months of my life. It's funny how all you really need is good company and some sunshine for the happiest memories.

The second lockdown wasn't so great. It was a cold, dark winter. My best friends who I lived with previously had graduated and moved away. I had just graduated with a degree in Psychology and Criminology, and I decided to continue studying a Masters in Forensic Psychology. Consequently, I was living in a studio flat on my own, where I also worked and did my Masters online. Spending all day, everyday there was lonely. I was quite depressed to be honest. I felt an emptiness I had never felt before and cried daily, not knowing why. Now I realise it was a lack of sunlight and human interaction!

On the bright side, I was lucky enough to have my boyfriend living in the same city this time. I stayed with him often and I had a few friends nearby so I wasn't completely alone, but it just felt like that some days.

With hindsight, I feel like this was a period of growth for me. Although at the time it seemed like my mental health had hit rock bottom, I was actually going through a transformation, becoming mentally stronger and more resilient than ever. When I think about it I realise that I no longer feel uncomfortable being alone with my thoughts and I experience a lot less anxiety than I used to. I have learnt to be comfortable with uncertainty, enjoy my own company and trust myself. Ever since that period, I have been extremely content with myself and my life. So I can thank the second lockdown for that opportunity to 'do the inner work', as they say. All in all, I had two very different experiences from the two lockdowns in England, but I've only taken good memories and lessons from them - I wouldn't change a thing.

Since 2020, I have been abroad about 8 times and I have 2 more holidays booked for this year. I haven't had any jabs. I personally did not think it was necessary, after doing my own research and a cost-benefit analysis of having them. I don't hold any extreme views against them, I just believe they are unnecessary and ineffective, and that in some cases they can do more harm than good. I don't judge other people for getting them - most of my friends and my boyfriend have had theirs. They all thought I was nuts at first for not getting mine, but over time they all understood and agreed with my decision. I have people around me who have had all their jabs just to travel, and know of others who haven't had any but won't go anywhere to avoid conforming to the restrictions in any way, whether that be buying a test or filling out a form.

I personally believe it's important to take control over your life, no matter what you believe in. I found loopholes to enable myself to travel when it was a difficult time to do so, and although I have had to take the odd test, I don't care about that too much. Everything is a cost-benefit analysis, after all!

I also now have my dream job in mental health - a field in which until recently, jabs were going to be made mandatory to work in. I think it is easy to fall victim to all this when you are in the minority, but I was not going to let the restrictions stop me from doing what I do best.

All things considered, I am happy with how my life has been over the past 2 years and with where I am right now - I don't think I am any worse off than I would have been if this pandemic hadn't happened.

Michelle

The world begins to open up
For our Golden boy Boo
Lockdown was hard
No formal training to do.

Now, slowly and surely
The process starts once more
Re-learning and repeating
Their confidence to restore.

New tasks and behaviour
Developing their skills
Building on Boo's foundation
Base of commands to instil.

Practice makes perfect
And it's certainly true
He's getting rather clever now
Our beautiful Boo.

His trainer 'Auntie Jo'
Who he utterly adores
Has worked with him since lockdown
Award-winning 'Applause for Paws'.

Loose-lead walking
Eye contact and respect
Settling and grounding
Teamwork takes effect.

Boo's also working through
A program of awards
Alongside other dogs
Reinforcement reaps rewards.

Correct handling and new concepts
He's so keen to please
Understanding and control
Observed by trainer Louise.

There's fun and play too
As he just loves to roam
Lots of woodland walks
It's become his second home!

Nose to the ground
He loves to explore
Oh how we love
Our adorable Labrador!

With special thanks to all the people who have supported Team Boo.

www.applauseforpawsdogtraining.co.uk
www.southcoastdogtrainingschool.co.uk

With trainer Jo

Alison

My Lockdown Journey Part Two

The world has gone mad. All the lies, confusion, deception, and fear have led to chaos through which non-sensical instructions, policies and happenings keep occurring. Out of chaos comes order but what type of order? Not the sort we all want, it would appear.

The government spouts lies and purposefully changes it's policies at a whim in order to create confusion and chaos, while behind closed doors it pushes through bills and acts that are designed to remove our freedoms, take our money and control our lives – enslaving us to them and their puppeteers.

People go about their everyday lives in disbelief, refusing to see, let alone believe, that they are walking blindly into a trap. A trap of control, enslavement, and ill health. The mainstream media continue to brainwash people through the black screens in their homes, their workplaces, their places of leisure, using tools such as NLP, Naomi and Ultra.

They have done such a good job that many people will never wake up to what is really going on and will continue to live in a world governed by fear, lies and deception. It is such a sad state of affairs and one I try hard not to think about.

Since the roll out of the Covid-19 injection the death rate has soared. People are dropping dead like flies, for no apparent reason - at least no reason that the government and mainstream media will admit to. Young, fit, healthy men and women in the prime of their lives just dropping dead in the streets, at the gym, on the pitch, on the court and even in their sleep... and they all have one thing in common. They have all had the Covid-19 genetic injection. Footballers, rugby players, tennis players, boxers, cyclists, motorists, and sportsmen and women from all sports, just dropping down dead. Before the rollout of the injection this would have been considered abnormal and a cause for concern.

Now, due to media brainwashing, this is considered normal. A new word has been invented for it, SADS (Sudden Adult Death Syndrome), except it's not a new word. SADS used to stand for seasonal affective disorder syndrome. They took an already familiar word and changed its meaning to suit their cover-up. The media went about using their hypnotic tools to convince people it is normal and acceptable so that they will continue to have the jab and put their lives in danger. The strength of the media's hypnotising abilities is so great that they have managed to persuade people that there is a war going on in Ukraine, despite the evidence otherwise, and that food, fuel and energy shortages are real, when they are not. The financial crisis, war and price hikes have all been manipulated by the government and played out by the mainstream media in order to bring in new controls and dependencies that would, under normal circumstances, not be accepted by the masses. Unwanted and un-needed taxes have been brought in in order to deprive the enslaved from their hard-earned money. Taxes that get squandered on things outside of this country for the benefit of the puppeteers and their puppets. People are squeezed to the point of deprivation and beyond, while those in power, party and live the life of Riley without even a glimpse of consideration for the harm they are creating.

Large corporations like Amazon, Facebook, Google, Black Rock, Vanguard, Ebay and PayPal all vie for the monopoly of their markets, squeezing out the small businesses, and controlling the products and information people receive. Banks control your account, your money and your online access. They decide who, they decide when and they decide how much you can pay, and they decide how much you can withdraw from your account. They have decided they do not need your permission to do anything or pay anyone. Banks operate in direct breach of GDPR by giving your personal details to third parties such as HMRC. They have also been known to withdraw amounts from your account to pay companies such as HMRC and councils, on their request and without direct debits or standing orders in place – a direct breach of GDPR and your fundamental rights.

Cash is being purposefully eroded away and enticements given to encourage people to switch to digital currency. Promises of a quicker, hassle free and hygienic means of paying for items and services has hoodwinked individuals and businesses into giving up their cash. By doing this people are handing over the control of their money to big corporations and third parties. Soon it will not be possible to hide your income or make transactions that are not traceable or taxable. The disposal of cash is another step in the direction of loss of freedom of choice. The banks already control who you pay and when.

How do I know all this? From research and life experiences of both myself and my friends. Life for the un-jabbed is not and has not been easy. We have had to deal with bullying, coercion, blackmail, discrimination, violence, assault – both verbal and physical in some cases, isolation, anger, and restrictions. Never in my life have I known any disease or vaccination cause all these discords and injustices.

So where am I now in all this? When I left you, in part one of my journey, I was coming out of the realisation phase and I was an emotional mess. Now I am in a state of numb acceptance. Just drifting along whatever path life has presented to me. I do not know where it is heading or what is in store for me. I do not care either. I have no fear of what is ahead, but I do have an expectancy of good and light. My journey is still travelling in darkness, but I have hope and I have optimism. Justified or not, only time will tell.

At the end of my story in book one, I was trying to find cures and help for those affected. I could not believe there was no hope for them but I have since had to face the fact that for some there is no hope. For those that have woken up to the reality of what is going on and have stopped having the jab there are things that can be taken to reverse the effects of the spike protein and graphene oxide found in the Covid-19 injections. For those who remain lost in fear and continue to take the poison I do not believe there is any hope.

The animals I so wanted to help I still want to help. The land I was hoping to find is currently out of my reach – prices are way too high, at present.

In December 2021 I qualified as a WEBB Bodywork for Animals Practitioner and use that, along with my animal healing qualification, to help animals in need. It breaks my heart just thinking about the huge flux of unwanted pets that is expected when the energy crisis properly kicks in this winter, so I try not to. The impact of the injections on animals health is visible to those whose eyes are open enough to see. Pets may not have received the injection but the effects of the shedding from their owners who have had the jab is sickening to watch. Pets are such loyal and devoted animals that love unconditionally, and to see them suffer due to the blind ignorance of their owners is sad to witness.

Shedding occurs when someone who has had a vaccine with a live sample in it passes the illness onto someone else. In the case of the Covid-19 injection you can't really call it shedding as the injection is not supposed to contain any live specimens. It is more like a transmission. A transmission of the harmful spike proteins (or maybe even something else) that gets into your bloodstream and makes you ill.

The un-jabbed are susceptible to this transmission from the jabbed, especially within the first three weeks of the injection being given. I have been transmitted on three times now, once in 2021 and twice this year, 2022. The jabbed do not see themselves as a threat to anyone. They believe it is the un-jabbed that are the threat. The effect of this transmitting is not pleasant to endure. The energy loss and the pain are almost too much to bear and can last for over a week. The latest bout did not fill my body with aches and pains in the way that it has in the past, so maybe I am building up a good immune response to it.

I do hope so as I refuse to cut the jabbed out of my life. It is not their fault they bought into the fear-mongering narrative or that they are carriers of a manmade virus that has been designed to do harm.

Before, during and after the first bout of transmission I was car booting with my sister. We do this every year to find new homes for items we no longer want. This year, the weather was kinder to us, so we were able to start the car boots in April. It is a tradition we started in 2013 when clearing out dad's home after he had passed away. Despite the early starts we both actually enjoy the experience and the quality time spent together.

Between the first and the second bout of illness, due to transmission I tried to start a 'Stand In the Park' in my home town of Westbury. It was unsupported and unattended by those who encouraged me to start it up, so I closed it after a couple of months. We were, by now, in the midst of autumn and I was suffering from a mild dose of depression. I was also entering my busy time of tax returns and year end deadlines... and Christmas was looming. Once again, I found myself working long hours trying to meet unrealistic deadlines and Christmas requirements. I spent Christmas and New Year with my sister and her husband, again. They are my closest relatives and great company. I love spending time with them. My brother and his family came and visited between Christmas and the New Year so we had a second Christmas celebration. It was lovely.

In January I succumbed to my second bout of transmission and found myself having to work to HMRC's deadline while in excruciating pain, and cursing the friend that had transmitted onto me. I remained bogged down with work until the end of June, having once again taken on a temporary contract that ran from April to end of June.

All rallies and roadside stands stopped for the whole of the period November to May. In May I went back to holding up the yellow boards on the A361 on a Saturday. It was good to be back getting the word out and mixing with like-minded people.

June was a whirr of work and dog sitting. Two different locations and four dogs, three in one place. It was a month of getting up between six and seven in the morning seven days a week and fitting deadline work in around dog walking. My stress levels were high, and my diet was not up to my usual standards, especially in the final two weeks when I had three dogs to walk that had a much more stringent routine.

For the first two weeks of June I was in the beautiful countryside of Symonds Yat. The cottage I stayed in was snuggled between hills and the river Wye. The walks varied between woodland, fields, and hills. The views were breath-taking and the dog was a dream to look after. My next two weeks were in Netheravon. The views were not as spectacular and the walks as interesting but it still had its beauty. It is hard not to find beauty in nature. The deadline work and the dog walking ended on the same weekend – the last one in June. I felt as if the weight of the world had been lifted from my shoulders. It was such a lovely feeling not having to chase deadlines.

July was spent catching up on other work, going to rallies and standing on the side of the A36 and A361 holding up yellow boards in an effort to wake people up to the truth of what is going on in the UK, the plans our government have for us and the fake news portrayed by the mainstream media. I also spent the month trying to catch up on everything that had been going on since the previous November. A tall order considering the speed at which everything was changing. I researched, wrote and delivered a talk on the current financial system, the tax fraud that is taking place, the national debt and presented ideas on how to prepare for the predicted financial crash. On top of this I started learning about Anna von Reitz and the Jural Assemblies. A very interesting subject that could turn out to be our salvation and the means through which we can save our planet and oust our corrupted governments.

In August I received my third bout of transmission. This time I did not have the pain I have had in the past. The energy loss was just as great though and the headache more prominent. I hope I do not have to go through this again but with the winter booster shots due, and already being rolled out to the vulnerable, I am not holding my breath.

This winter is looking as if it is going to be very tough for many people. A financial crash is predicted for the autumn, fuel prices, food prices and energy prices are expected to skyrocket. This is expected to drive people and businesses to bankruptcy and force individuals onto universal credit. Many are likely to become homeless. Many more will be seeking out food banks and heat banks in order to survive. All this on top of the flu jab and coronavirus booster. What  chance do people have? I just hope that light prevails and prevents most of this from happening. For the sake of every living thing.

I do believe with all my heart that good will win in the end and all this suffering will become a distant memory.

WhatKnot

Crisp Winter

Starry Night

Raffia

hine On

Bob

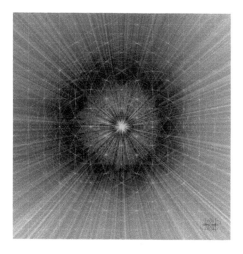

I am not going into the politics of the measures taken; that is a whole other subject!

In early 2020 when we first heard the news about this strange virus that had just been discovered, the rumours were that it was either a death sentence escaped from some laboratory, or another Flu virus that just mutates every year.

We were quite prepared to go through it, the same as every other year!

It soon became the most talked about topic on Facebook, and all other social media, and I started to listen to health specialists to see how I could best protect myself, and I knew that keeping a healthy immune system was going to be half the battle.

I took the advice that viruses can't stand high temperatures, and if we found ourselves with viral symptoms, we were recommended to drink something as hot as we could bear, and continue regularly until the symptoms disappeared. This would melt the protein shell of the virus whilst it was still in the nasal passageways, where it resided until it had multiplied and moved. Prevent it from getting down to the airways. This apparently is applicable to all viruses!

I have always endeavoured to eat healthy foods which worked in my favour because we were reminded that eating healthily boosts the immune system.

I had always suffered from the Flu inoculations, and have declined them for quite a few years since I lost a whole Christmas because of the effects, so I decided to follow the above procedures rather than have the inoculation on offer. I have a history of lung problems, so you can see why I was particularly interested to get it right. Yes! I did get a virus and it was unlike any other virus or flu I had ever had before, and, yes, it was horrible! But I am over seventy and still alive and glad that I didn't choose to take chemicals.

The Panic had started! Restrictions had been introduced, fortified by the Spanish police. Stores were closing. Our family business relied on a particular brand of stores, which got more and more restricted and eventually closed. That was the business truncated to a survival level.

When the Lockdown prevented anyone from doing anything outside the house, we all filled our time with other things. I had become interested in digital art, and it was a grand moment to really dig in and see what I could do. I would post something every day; be it a short video, or an artwork and this gave me an impetus to stretch!

I discovered my *Art Habit!*

Through that and connections with other art groups I developed a greater understanding of art and my own capabilities.

You might think that this may be a bit bizarre - but, it was like Mrs King in my primary class trying to teach me to spell 'a' - suddenly something clicks!

I feel that art was the only benefit I got from Lockdown. I suppose that what I'm trying to say is that every change has an effect on everything! My life has changed completely since the first lockdown in March 2020 and art has been my Lockdown saviour. I have a couple of pages in the book of my last artworks.

Looking back over the last years I realise I have lost a whole way of life, but, as the Monty Python team would say... "Always Look On The Bright Side!"

JB

My Take On Lockdown

"You know when you roll up to a gig and the stage is too small, not enough power, bad get in, what do you do? Adapt and carry on. That's what us three did."

I'm 72 and pensioned, a retired roadie/wireman, and worked in the care industry. My partner Tina is 60, worked for the Body Shop and now on the railways, Tina continued working because the trains didn't stop.

Our son Jack is 25 and lives in Lewes, now a musician/actor and his day job is a mentor at a fundraising organisation in Brighton. During lockdown Jack was furloughed on 70% wages. Jack completed Uni in 2018 and the following year he did

'Camp America' as a guitar teacher where he met and befriended loads of fellow players from all over. During lockdown he was in contact on the net with many of them, usually late evening for a couple of hours. To celebrate the end of lockdown, four of his ex-flat mates at Uni climbed Ben Nevis. "Let's do something positive" they said.

The roads were quiet, the weather was good. Jack played endless guitar and is pretty good now. I bought a microphone and recorded birdsong on our many walks.

My Mum died, not Covid related. I supported my Dad and still do, as the loss of his wife after 72 years is life-changing for him.

I didn't buy into any of the conspiracy theories cause I wrote them off as bollocks. I don't believe in outside devious sources that are trying to fuck me up.

I'm pretty up to speed on politics and capitalism, I've studied it and none of it is fair or perfect, I have no illusions. Education doesn't tell you what to think, it gives you the tools to work it out yourself.

The one thing that could have fucked me up would have been lack of money or a pile of debts. We three in our house are sound on that front. So no big deal over here in West Sussex.

Roll with the punches.

Alasdair & Lydia Walker-Cox

GRITTY FAITH

'May the Lord Himself establish you in His best purposes for you. May He strengthen you with holy conviction and gritty faith to climb every mountain He's assigned to you. May He increase your capacity to love and encourage others. And when the enemy rises up against you, may you see with your own eyes how God fights for you. You're on the winning side. You can rest.'

The words above were taken from a calendar I had given a friend of ours as a gift. This friend sent me these words because they were on the very date of our crown court appeal. We were appealing against a conviction and fines we'd been given in the magistrates court the previous August. Our crime was that we refused to close our business during lockdowns 2 and 3 on the basis that we've always sold food. Our local council, Wychavon, would not accept that we fell under the 'food retailer' exemption as they didn't feel we sold enough or the right kind of food. The fines and costs had reached a staggering £44,000!

The days, weeks and months between our conviction in August and the appeal date in February had their highs and lows. We have faith in a loving Creator God and knew he'd never leave us throughout this ordeal. There were times, though, of doubts and fears about the possibility of having those huge fines to pay, plus more added on from the court of appeal if we lost the case.

We were determined to represent ourselves in court as we felt the legal team that we had at the trial let us down. A good solicitor friend of ours felt very strongly that we should have legal representation. Being a very stubborn person, and feeling that we knew our business better than anyone, we held to our independent position. Our friend did manage to persuade us to make use of a newly qualified barrister he knew to help us out. I only wanted his assistance in a McKenzie capacity. This wonderful young lad would only charge us a nominal fee for his help which was amazing. He only came on board with our case 2 weeks before the appeal date, so we didn't have much time to make him familiar with all the intricacies of what had happened to date.

So, the morning of 25th February arrived. On that morning we received the words I began this chapter with, and we felt this was a promise from Father God that we would be on the winning side! This certainly didn't give us a glib feeling, but we felt the rest that comes with trust placed in someone outside of ourselves.

We met up with our barrister friend an hour or so before the court case started. This was the first time we'd met in person. We warmed to Josh very quickly and could tell immediately that he was extremely competent and had empathy with our situation. So just half an hour to go before having to go into court, I asked Josh if he could actually represent us rather than simply be a McKenzie Friend. He said he would have to ask the judge if this was ok as it was all last minute. The judge was happy for Josh to go ahead with representing us. It seemed to us that he thought it was good that this newly qualified barrister was getting some work experience!

The case took all day to be heard as we had to trawl through everything again. Finally, though, the judge returned from discussing the case with his 2 magistrate judges who had been either side of him throughout. The result was an immense relief to my husband and I. On a point of law and a point of fact, the judge allowed us to win the appeal. "You are free to go" was music to our ears and we left not having to pay a penny to the court. Josh was able to put in a claim for his costs which was greatly deserved on his part.

At the time of writing this there are many reports emerging detailing the harms that lockdowns have caused. There have been huge consequences on mental health, missed health check-ups, economic hardship and much much more.

We actually terminated our 30 year business in April of this year. Business had been decreasing for the last 10 years and the 'lockdown years' had been the final nail in the coffin. We took advantage of a break clause in the lease and closed the shop. Another empty unit in our town centre! The landlords were uninterested in giving us any incentive to stay.

It has been a great relief to no longer be running a struggling retail business in an increasingly quiet town centre. My husband was often working 70 hours a week for not much return for his efforts.

We are looking forward to a very different Christmas this year than we've been used to. Days off over the festive period were usually Christmas Day, Boxing Day & New Year's Day. This year we are looking forward to lots of family time!

One incredibly positive outcome of no longer having the shop and all it's responsibilities, is that I've be even able to give a lot more of my time to supporting my Dad in his care of Mum. Mum is extremely challenging as she has Alzheimer's. I now have her at home with me for 12+ hours a week which gives Dad significant respite. There's always a lot going on in our home and the stimulation is good for Mum. Our little granddaughter, who's two and a half now, is often here while our daughter is at work. She's expecting another baby, due in April next year, so that's exciting for us all. Mum loves being with children, it reminds her of her training and jobs as a nursery nurse. We have so much to be thankful for!

We turn our faces now to different challenges. Life will always have it's challenges. It's wonderful to face these knowing that Jesus has promised His followers *'Lo, I am with you always, even to the end of the age'. (Matthew 28 v 20)*

Ken Strauss

As soon as they announced lockdown in Spain I knew something was amiss. The way to survive Covid is with a strong immune system, and the best way to maintain it is through aerobic physical exercise (which was now impossible confined in our houses). So I found a dozen little ways to cheat without putting myself or anyone else at risk.

Living in an area with lots of forest paths nearby, we began to walk our dog about 17 times a day. Previously the dog had ample space to run around in the yard, but now he was out on every tree-lined trail we could find. Our Golden, Jimmy, was in seventh heaven.

I also started making my house calls by bike instead of car, and I trekked up and down a mountain to get to the hospital in Dénia from my home some 10 km away, an aerobic delight. The police would often stop me but I always had my stethoscope and doctor's license in my backpack. I was amazed how quickly people became little fascists. I was stopped once in the woods by another dog walker. This Swiss man whom I'd never met accosted me face-to-face, without a mask, because I was using a retractable leash instead of an ordinary one. He said the authorities had forbidden them. When I pointed out that his dog wasn't even on a leash he said that it didn't matter. The principle stood.

Once, when a police woman stopped me and I asked her to put on a mask (hers was dangling below her chin) she nearly arrested me. (Spanish police were told to impose huge fines for any sign of 'insolence'.) Then she asked me to take mine off so she could identify me by matching my exposed face to my ID photo.

At first, when I biked by, people would shout at me from balconies: 'Get yourself home. You're spreading germs.' I went to biking with my white coat on and a stethoscope around my neck. Then they cheered and banged pans when I rode by. That was at the beginning. By the end of lockdown I was getting eggs thrown at me. Somehow the fact I was a doctor was nothing to cheer about any more.

Julia Evans

Time can never stand still, change comes - the dusk must travel through the night to find the dawn.

For me this time has been about transformation. This whole two and a half years have been a transition. I feel we are collectively transforming.

On some level all of us have had to face loss - the loss of a loved one; the loss of freedom; the loss of a business; the loss of a relationship; the loss of freedom.

My own personal story has been complex and has many layers but at the root of each layer is the subject of loss. Rather than telling my story I would like to give you some hope, something to think about - we have all been on a path of transformation.

I would like to use a card in the tarot deck as a metaphor of this loss. One of my favourite cards in the tarot deck, believe it or not is the death card. It is a card that can often strike fear and a sense of foreboding. But I feel it is a very misunderstood card and one that can actually be very beautiful.

For me this card symbolises transformation. In order for anything to change something has to die, has to end. We must remove the old, the things that are not serving us to make space for the new. Like the caterpillar that turns into a butterfly, the cocoon stage is dark. But I have learnt that sometimes we must walk through the darkness to get to the light.

Transformation is never easy, change is never easy. Sometimes we choose the path of transformation ourselves, but more often than not we are thrust into the darkness, we have not made the decision to do so ourselves but change is forced upon us and something we love dearly is taken away. We suddenly find ourselves there, laying in a black abyss. It can be lonely, it can be cold and hard.

So this is for anybody out there who feels like they are scrambling alone in the dark. I have been there many times and I am down there with you as I write these words.

But this is not a post of despair, these are not words of sadness. This is to remind you that light will always shine in the dark. This is to remind you that after every death comes birth. After every end comes a new beginning. To promise you that when you step back into the light you will not recognise yourself, because if you allow it, the cocoon is the best place to transform, to find a YOU that you never knew existed and to discover a strength that you never had.

And be sure to know - you do not have to lie in the dark, it is possible to dance in the darkness… I do.

The Moth

Death sits and waits on the wings of the moth.
She stills the turmoil that jilted minds seek.
Only through the darkest door can we taste the mouth of change,
as transformation summons us to the depths of light.

Michael Flannagan

After-effect - August 2022

It took nearly two years, but we managed to get through the pandemic. Sitting at home trying to sort through all the madness, wondering if life will ever be the same will probably occupy my thoughts for decades to come. The dark prophecies warned us that nothing would be the same, so in a way, we were not surprised. Hearing that should make things easier to bear, but knowledge doesn't always make things less complicated.

There isn't as much talk about COVID these days. In Germany, we still must wear masks on public transportation, which is good because readjustment takes time. It would be folly to think everything would miraculously be normal without the discomfort of transition; the human psyche doesn't work that way, which is why I'm a bit skeptical of crowds, or if people cough in closed spaces, but that, too, is normal. When the fear creeps up my spine like a deceptive serpent, I tell myself to breathe deeply and trust life because it is, in every aspect, on our side.

Two significant things stay with me and occupy my thoughts daily.

Firstly, I never imagined how politicised human health could be until COVID. We've heard about the money-making schemes within the world of big pharma. It tore something inside of me as I watched politicians willing to jeopardise lives because one party said this, and they said that. I watched and shook my head as governors went before federal judges to block mask-wearing in schools, in hospitals, and in the middle of a worldwide pandemic, how Senators and Representatives worked their supporters up to the point of wishing death on health officials who were only doing what they thought was best for the public's safety. Now that COVID is over, how I view politics has changed enormously.

Secondly, and more importantly, never have I been so convinced of the importance of art. Never have I been more certain that artists: jugglers, clowns, musicians, actors, writers, cooks, and dancers, are the true backbone of every society - not the bankers, brokers, and engineers. I am not lessening their worth, but COVID brought a lot into perspective. Society has ingrained in us that these crazy artists are a burden, but it wasn't the bankers, the checks that helped people buy groceries that encouraged the masses, but a song, music, dance, and poetry. It wasn't the stock market that healed communities after death, but the artists.

Let an artist stand on the ruins in war-torn cities and towns, and it will mobilise countries.

Amid devastation and hopelessness, no one needs to hear how the economy is thriving, nor is anyone concerned about the current gas price. We need something that transports hope when hanging on by a thread that could snap at any moment. Art is the language that does not need interpretation because it travels in the realm that connects humankind. The world needs us as life needs breath. Every artist, whether he fills the most celebrated halls, sings a soft song or traces the silhouette of a flower for a child, regardless of the medium, is unique and saves the world daily.

The world would not survive without our crazy, wild, chaotic, beautiful contribution.

Kat

Why can't you just be normal?

According to various government health advisors and President Biden (who promised that the unvaccinated were facing a winter of sickness and almost certain death) - I shouldn't be alive and well enough to write this little update to my life. However, good news for me and not such good news for profit hungry pharmaceutical companies, I'm extremely healthy and also feeling a lot more positive than I was at the beginning of, what I perceive as, the hysterical worldwide Covid lockdown extravaganza in March 2020.

Having defiantly refused to wear masks, sanitise my hands, stay away from friends and family and queue up obediently for 1/2/3/4 jabs, I certainly went against the tide in the early days but I've noticed a slow shift in narrative and now, when even MP's are competing against each other as to whom objected the earliest and loudest about Covid lockdown policies, I do feel there might be a delicious 'Told you so' moment in my future. But if there isn't, then that's fine too because this whole experience has given me more confidence in my convictions and made me a more robust person - 'What doesn't kill you makes you stronger' etc... It's also taught me that the government, the media and pharmaceutical companies are conflicted and do not really have my or my family's best interests at heart. It is therefore my sole responsibility to make informed decisions for myself and my children. I hope that my children will barely register the peculiar homeschooling blip in their life and be proud of having the only parent at the nativity play who could actually smile warmly at them in a sea of otherwise identically obedient masked half faces.

Over the past couple of years the world seems to have split into two camps of either putting on a bit of lockdown weight or exercising excessively to use the time productively, get out of homeschooling, take out frustrations with Joe Wicks or on the pavement. I was an 'exercise excessively' type - to the point of damaging my ankle running, which has never quite recovered. I'm now a cardio kick boxing addict and have a set up both in the garden (apologies to my neighbours for the sweaty grunting) and in the kids 'playroom' - the lego and crayons now having to share space with dumbbells, resistance bands and a Pilates ball. I was determined to enter my 40's at peak physical fitness and also held aspirations to get a 6-pack. My youngest daughter likes to sweetly ask me why it's called a 6-pack when I "only have 4". Only!

I also started a love affair with motorbikes, spurred on from listening to the bikers whizzing around on the empty roads and having that thing that a fearful population aren't supposed to have... FUN! I decided to go to the children's sports day on my motorbike, not realising how tremendously embarrassing this was going to be for my eldest daughter who asked in despair "Why can't you just be normal?" I asked what constituted normal and she said "Arriving in a car like everyone else" and also "baking a cake". So 'a motorbike-riding, non-baking, just about (if she tenses) has a 4-pack Mum'. #embarrassing.

I'm still flying around the world for work - although of course some countries are still sadly out of bounds to un-jabbed even when the science clearly indicates said jabs are barely effective, and if so only for a very short time. By and large the world has gone mostly back to normal although I feel this is less by decree and more by people not caring about the 'rules' anymore and realising that they are largely unenforceable.

Perhaps one of the last legacies of Covid will be the intricate hotel policy of cleaning the TV remote control and putting it in a little sterilised bag for your safety. Much like putting miniature liquids in a sandwich bag to go through airport security, 20 years will pass and no one will remember why it was we started doing it in the first place.

I've heard a theory that our planet serves as the lunatic asylum for the rest of the universe and I've been wondering how I'm going to survive the next half of my life here on our crazy little woke world. I've decided that, despite what my daughter wishes, I think it's actually best not to be normal, even if that leaves you in a minority of one. But, equally, constantly raging against the machine and being wildly livid is exhausting (cardio boxing does help alleviate this). I am an irrelevant cog in an enormously powerful machine whose momentum I cannot stop.

Whilst I am relieved at my decision to trust my immune system and to protect my children from 'Big Pharma', what everyone else chooses to do may sadden me but I no longer take it on as my burden. The friends I have lost, courtesy of the pandemic (emotionally lost) will probably never come back - I don't believe they were ever truly afraid of my maskless face and unsanitised hands, I think it was being faced with strength and resilience that was off-putting.

There have been studies done on resilience and which personality type is more likely to survive challenging circumstances. It's not the pessimist and, perhaps more surprisingly, neither is it the optimist. It's the middle of the road person who believes that whilst tomorrow may well be grim, and perhaps the day after that too, ultimately, sometime in the future, good will prevail. This is what I believe so all I can do in the meantime is never comply to having my freedoms curtailed by gormless scientists and their fantastical charts. And since we find ourselves cohabiting on the nominated galactic crazy planet I shall do all this with a broad and genuine smile on my maskless face. I'm mad, you're mad, we're all mad - so let's at least be kind to each other.

Stay Wild Moon Child

Terri and Colin

Terri, Susi and Colin

We live in Melbourne, the most locked down place on earth. Feels strange to say that as my memories of the past 2 and a half years are very mixed.

We are of the age – late 60's at the beginning of 2020 – when we are theoretically vulnerable to all sorts of things. It did cause a bit of consternation, especially at the outset of the pandemic when so much was not known, and there was, paradoxically a huge amount of information about it.

The first lockdown was a complete lockdown, although we were not sealed into our houses like some in China, and other places. We wore masks all the time; watched endless news conferences (and Netflix); fretted about infection numbers and the capacity of the health system and the atrocities in the nursing homes; and scowled at those who were stockpiling toilet paper; or refused to wear masks (or walking with empty coffee cups so they didn't have to wear masks) or were demonstrating.

We also praised our Premier, and congratulated the Federal Government for their measures to supplement the incomes of those who had lost their employment, and there were very many of them. The excessive use of police force to break up demonstrations was not a great look. In a later lockdown, a Council Block was sealed up for a number of days, which incurred wrath from many of the population and a huge amount of community support and activity. They were given virtually no notice, so could not prepare in any way.

It is amazing how rapidly things unravelled. Personal routines – like going to the gym - were replaced by other activities. Social routines were replaced by less social activities. The activities of the society imploded and one breakdown led to another, showing us how interconnected everything is – both nationally and internationally.

We walked in empty streets, having a dog allowed us to exercise her. Everyone else in our suburb also had a dog, or quickly acquired one, so we always ran into people in the street. People were a lot friendlier. There were no cars, no airplanes. Creepy.

The shopping centre was deserted and most of the shops were closed. It did feel like a post apocalypse movie. We had to do our own hair!! Many went grey during this time, and some soldiered on doing their own roots (me). Later on, trading was permitted on a click and collect basis – and some of the life returned. But it was quite desolate for a while there - no cinemas, restaurants, library, bridge club, bowling. Then, there was takeaway coffee and people 'bumping into' each other and chatting. Also, more beggars in our suburb!

But: there was far less pollution, and we could see all the way across the Bay and see the towers of Melbourne as clear as clear, and the water was clear and beautiful. Not all bad then.

On a personal note, we are two elderly introverts, who get on very well together. Our need for people is limited. We also were able to bear the changes financially. Quite fortunate really. There were many for whom that was not the case. Colin started making sourdough bread – the true lockdown cliché – and started baking. Everyone became obsessed with food. I cleaned out the kitchen cupboards.

We were unable to go to our regular market – limited to 5km radius of travel in the 2nd and subsequent lockdowns. However, we arranged for one of the traders to deliver to us. And we live in a well-appointed part of the city so food was not the biggest issue.

Netflix got a big workout, zoom dinners with friends, meeting up with very chatty neighbours over the fence and always keeping a distance, online bridge tournaments (the technology improved quickly during this time), online Pilates classes and several thousand games of 'Words with Friends' - kept me plugged in, kind of.

I was not aware of how it had affected me until the restrictions were lifted. The first time we went out I felt naughty and transgressive. Going places still makes me nervous, crowds especially. Some of my friends will still not go to some places – restaurants, theatres etc. We have all become more inward looking.

There are staff shortages everywhere, especially in the retail and hospitality industries. So, hours are cut, and service isn't what it was. Hotels are operating differently. Travel is a mess and flying is a lottery. Many businesses have not reopened. Hospitals are under a great deal of pressure from understaffing and demand.

We are still getting reports of numbers of infection in the news. They are still telling us to wear masks everywhere inside. We have had 4 injections (2 shots and 2 boosters) and both of us got Covid. It was not terrible but not great, and I had residual brain fog, and exhaustion that lasted 6 weeks after I recovered – it still hangs on a bit.

The lockdowns did get tedious – although everyone was finding 'workarounds' to keep within restrictions - however, not everyone did. Some people changed their official residence to their holiday home so they could get out of the city. My last two birthdays were in lockdown – so no celebrations or visits from friends.

The main thing is, that like everyone else, we feel cheated out of 2 and a half years of our lives. It is as if there is a big hole in our experience. There is pre Covid and post Covid, and the middle bit is a blank, no memories, no experiences really. Given our age we feel that there is not that much time to compensate and recover ahead, and there is the pity.

Veronica

Hello again!

After reading everyone's wonderful stories in Book 1, I was inspired to write a more 'complete' personal account of the last two years, and so, here it is!

In late February and early March 2020, when I first became aware of COVID-19 (or 'the coronavirus' as it was more commonly referred to in those early days), and the news coming out of China, I was extremely concerned.

My family and I were living in Melbourne at that time, for context. I began to check the World Coronavirus Map everyday, which was a site that kept track of daily virus cases in each country, and felt my anxiety rise when cases in Spain started to increase, as I am from Spain and half my family lives there, including elderly relatives.

For years I had been planning to go back to Spain to visit my family after I finished High School at the end of 2020, and I was terrified I wouldn't be able to do so. My parents became diligent about sanitising, and told me we weren't going to be leaving the house unless we absolutely couldn't avoid it. Tensions were high. Everyone was waiting; waiting for the first cases in Australia, waiting for schools to be shut and for lockdown to be implemented.

I wrote in my diary a lot, in that first month. Reading it now, it's pretty surreal just how much fear my family and I felt. I was so worried, so convinced this would be the end of life as we knew it, that millions of people would die and our world would be plunged into chaos. Of course, in the end, it was the end of normal life, but not for the reasons I had first thought.

I mention this first chunk of time to truly highlight the fear I had in the beginning, and to show that I… well… changed my mind. Originally, I really did believe in the 'evidence' and 'trusted the science', and all of that. I wasn't always sceptical. I fell for it hook, line and sinker. So when I started to realise all was not what it seemed, it was a very gradual process, and it was very difficult to swallow.

There was never really an 'a ha!' moment, never a moment where everything just clicked and I started to see things differently. At least, not that I can remember. All I know is that by April 2020, once we'd been in lockdown for several weeks longer than those initial 'two weeks to flatten the curve!' - something began to not sit right with me. By June 2020, I was completely against lockdowns, all mandates, and most of the measures taken. The hypocrisy of the BLM protests in America, in particular, being celebrated and encouraged while at the same time any freedom/ anti-mandate/anti-lockdown protests were condemned for being 'dangerous, super-spreader events' stands out as something that really cemented how ridiculous it was all getting.

Gradually, little by little, I shifted from simply believing governments were being power hungry and deliberately taking advantage of the pandemic to exert more power, to understanding the true reality of the bigger picture. How it was all planned from the very beginning. How it's not the governments who are in power, but a group of very powerful and incredibly evil beings working from the shadows, who control almost every aspect of our lives, and have been for at least hundreds of years. How the 'pandemic' was merely one step in their plan to completely destroy our current way of living, our society, in order to build a new world – a new world benefiting only them – from the ashes of it. What they are currently doing, and what they plan to do, is absolutely horrific, and perhaps not appropriate to cover right now, so I won't. But if you know, you know. It has never been more evident that we are at war, and that there is still so, so much we don't understand about our reality.

I did not want to accept this at first. I was freshly 18, with dreams and plans for the future, trying to finish my last year of High School. I did everything I could to disprove it, to dismiss it as lies, but in the end, the evidence was, and is, simply too great, and I knew in my heart that it was true.

I'm still not sure why, exactly, I was able to break free from the spell. Perhaps it is because I have always been open to new ideas, new perspectives, and have never been someone swayed by public opinion, or someone who cares what other people think of me. Perhaps, too, it is because I am surrounded by family and friends with views that go against the mainstream. Either way, though it has been a curse in many ways to know (ignorance, as they say, truly is bliss), I do not regret being aware of what is going on.

The second half of 2020, and most of 2021, was extremely difficult for me emotionally. Knowing what I know was extremely isolating. I lost my connection and closeness to my friends, all of whom refused to see reason. Everywhere I went, people were calling me crazy and dangerous. I coped through humour, through joining communities of likeminded people, and from knowing that it didn't matter what other people thought, because the truth was the truth (bear in mind that I say 'truth', but what I really mean is 'the closest thing to the truth', because at the end of the day, none of us will ever really know everything, and there is still so much that is hidden from us). But for many months, I was, in many ways, not just suffering through the emotional burden of knowing, and the lockdowns and jab mandates that still continued, but grieving. Grieving what I'd lost in the past year due to lockdowns, yes, which I already covered in Book 1, but mostly... grieving the loss of the future I'll never get to have. I grieved the fact that I hadn't been able to go to Spain – my home, where I'd lived half my life, and that I missed so, so much – and that realistically, I probably never would.

I'm now 20 years old, and for me, everyday life has mostly gone back to 'how it was before'. For others, not so much. As a society, we are on the knife's edge. Everything is going according to plan. The next few years – and really, the rest of our lifetimes, however long they end up being – are going to be extremely difficult. But for at least this last little while, in this calm before the storm, I've been able to pretend.

It is incredibly frustrating, though, to have everybody begin to realise and talk about the detrimental impact of lockdowns now when I – and many others – were warning about it as early as

May 2020. Oh, who could have possibly foreseen all these extremely serious social issues? Certainly not us! Lockdowns were the only option! "We had no idea the effects were going to be so bad!" they say, and it's such bullshit. We knew damn well what they would do from the very beginning. I was labelled a lunatic for saying so two years ago! I'm not sure what is worse, thinking none of this was foreseeable, or knowing it was but believing lockdowns were justified, anyway. I now live in a new city, Brisbane, which only had around 60 days of lockdown in total, compared to the over 250 days we had in Melbourne, and it was nowhere near as hard of a lockdown at any point in time compared to what we faced. A lot of people here don't understand what it was like. They have no concept of it. They just brush it aside, like "Haha, yeah, lockdown, that silly old thing." It was NOT silly. It was horrific. It was a stripping of our freedoms and rights; freedoms and rights that the government had no right to take away from us for any reason, no matter what.

One of the many good traits of the human race is our adaptability; we adapt very quickly and very well to new situations, but it is also a curse. People have gotten used to this. The precedent has been set. People will accept whatever manufactured crisis comes next. Even for those of us who lived in Melbourne, the general feeling among us is of… forgetting. People have forgotten how bad it really was. Myself and my family have found ourselves forgetting, and we lived through it – all 250+ days of lockdown – while being completely against it!

There is a sense of slightly hysterical disbelief when we think back. We weren't allowed to travel more than 5km from our homes for months! We had a curfew! I wasn't allowed to go to school for half the year! People were facing tens of thousands of dollars in fines if they didn't have a weekly permit to go to work! It was – and is – disgusting. We can't help but laugh, because if we don't, we just end up crying.

Right now I'm in my first year of university, and I'm enjoying it quite a lot, but again… there is that disconnect, because most people here don't know what it was like and can never understand. They continue to be blissfully unaware of the impeding global crises.

Sometime around the end of 2021 and the start of this year (2022), my mentality began to shift. I am still extremely saddened by all that I lost in 2020, and all that I've lost in the future – though that hasn't happened yet, and I try not to think about it too much these days in fear of falling into a deep well of depression. There are things I will never, ever get back, and I continue to stand by the fact that I will never forgive those who are putting us through this. But now… now my anger and grief has shifted, somewhat. Not to acceptance, but to simply… pushing it aside, because I can't afford to dwell on it any longer. I can't. There is too much going on.

I need to focus on the present. I need to enjoy the little time I have left of relative normality and appreciate the things in life we've always taken for granted. A home. A family. Good food. Clean water. The internet. Cars. Hot showers.Stability. Whilst also thinking to the future, not with anger and hurt, but simply matter-of-factly, while at the same time preparing myself mentally to be able to endure all that is coming. And, very importantly, without losing hope.

The situation is bleak. Incredibly bleak. But I wouldn't still be here if I thought there was no hope whatsoever that those who wish to destroy us might one day fail.

I'll end on some positive news. Due to a small window of opportunity offered up to me in May this year, when the Australian

Government allowed those of us not jabbed to leave the country after over a year of closed borders, I was incredibly fortunate to be able to return to Spain for a few weeks, and see my family. I truly thought I never would, and yet... I did. Still can't believe it, to be honest!

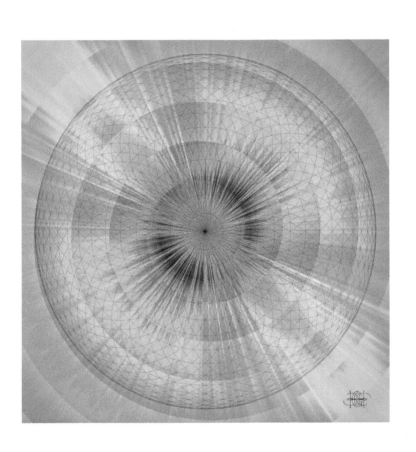

Bill and Linda Hurren

In March 2020 we were with friends in Lanzarote celebrating Bill's birthday; we are both in our 70's and like to spend time in a warmer climate, especially in the winter. On that evening we were watching the news and hearing about this new disease that seemed to be travelling the world. We all thought - "Oh dear, the newscasters are obviously struggling to find something to talk about - it's winter and there is always flu and bugs about so get over it."

On returning to the UK we began to think again - the wonderful Care Home where my Mum was living closed their doors to everybody and that was devastating for both her and our family. On 16th March it was her 97th birthday and I was not allowed in to see her. The Home had taken the decision to close prior to the UK being shutdown, that was terrible... for as many years as

I can remember I always saw my Mum on her birthday.

We delivered presents to the Home and I wrote a card trying to explain the situation - but by this time we were all becoming concerned as we were in complete lockdown, something none of us had ever experienced before and in fact quite frightening and very unnerving. In the UK, lockdown was nothing like it was in Lanzarote, so in some respects we were glad to be home.

Although we weren't there, we heard Lanzarote lockdown meant – only 1 person at a time allowed out for a walk, 1 person out in the car to go to the supermarket, the seafront was cordoned off so no one could walk on it. People queued in the street for the bank and chemist and could only go in one at a time. Mum's Home was brilliant, they started to allow visits behind a closed window which was really good for normal people, but for my Mum who was stone deaf it was not easy. She didn't understand and she kept saying it was as if she was in prison. We then started having zoom calls - brilliant for some people but hard work for others. It was hard work for us with Mum unable to hear. I do a lot of sewing so I started to take pictures of the things I was sewing and I typed up everything I would have said to her on a visit in large font. Sitting at home, on a zoom call, I sat in front of the computer holding up everything I had written for her to read and holding up the photos of my sewing so she could see what I was doing. Mum would read and reply accordingly; it was lovely to find this way to communicate and wonderful that she was up to speed with what we were doing, or not doing as was the case! I feel quite confident Mum understood what this terrible virus was all about and I also think she understood 'lockdown' as we wrote everything down explaining what was going on for her to read. I had

previously visited Mum every day of the week and on the odd occasions we were lucky enough to go away, we had a wonderful circle of friends who were happy to visit her.

In June 2020 just as we were settling back into our daily routine of visiting Mum, even though it was by an open door or in the summer house, it was still wonderful for both of us, we were dealt another lockdown blow - this fantastic Care Home announced they were changing ownership. This was devastating news to me as we had built such an excellent relationship with all the staff and indeed with the owners. However, with our best foot forward we moved on staying very positive and found the new owner was a tall, dark and handsome young man who proved to be lovely and very caring. Mum's comment on him was "What a lovely young man he was, great shame about his brown shoes, but nonetheless a lovely young man!" Covid continued to take hold in every country of the world.

Sadly Mum had a fall on the 29th of October and ended up in hospital where she had a bionic screw put in her hip at the age of 97 years and 6 months. She died within a month of this traumatic experience. We were only allowed 30 people at the funeral, all wearing masks wet from the tears. It has been very difficult to move on and get closure. The new owner and all his staff were so very very kind and supportive, especially when Mum died. The owner and five members of staff attended the funeral which we thought was amazing, especially in lockdown. A lovely positive memory of lockdown has been how some staff have kept in touch with us to this day and have really become friends, knowing how loved and respected Mum was by everybody at the Home helps us get closure.

On the day Mum died, England announced they had found a vaccine - that to us was excellent news, we both wanted the jab as soon as it was available - we accept there are people who don't trust it, but we do. We certainly think we have so far escaped Covid and trust we will continue to do so. We both had our 4th jab in April and will hopefully be getting a 5th jab in the autumn.

Lockdown for some people has been terrible and indeed very lonely, however we feel that we may be coming out the other side now especially with the jabs available.

We have a lot of faith in our NHS and the jabs, and while there are people who don't and won't agree I think the majority will agree. We started doing 'doorstep food drops' to help friends who were very poorly at home, we felt so very sorry for people who were suffering alone, some of whom were elderly with nobody to help them. We are members of local charities and one does what one can, but we feel very strongly that people should bite the bullet and do what they can to help themselves by getting the jab.

Skye Coelho

2022: The Great Shift and the Wild Mountain Woman!

"Greetings from an isolated caravan in the Spanish mountains."

In February 2022 I had taken myself away from daily life to work through the deep trauma and grief that occurred during 2020/2021 and disconnect from the global madness, or so I thought!

My plan was that solitude and nature combined would aid in bringing me back to a greater sense of balance and healing. That was until I received the news from my friend in Ukraine. Once again, I was drawn back to the global insanity and chaos, instantly triggered into a state of anxiety and fear of losing yet another loved one.

I have a good friend living in the centre of Kyiv who sadly returned to his home country last year, 2021, to rebuild his life having fled the previous Ukrainian conflict to begin a new life in Spain. He, like many others had to return to his home country due to the economic and health consequences of the pandemic which have had far reaching effects, most of which are not yet apparent.

War games are nothing new of course, throughout the pandemic/ lockdown we had been discussing the next potential major conflicts, where the power struggle would ultimately lead us - China/Taiwan, Russia/Ukraine amongst the most dangerous, more obvious possibilities with their global consequences. However, when you have a personal connection, everything changes despite the wise words of a friend, 'observe not absorb'.

My initial idea of taking time out from any internet usage was momentarily scuppered as I had constant contact with my friend and updates from the situation in his country, which led me to write the article, Ukraine: The Consequences of War in Pandemic Times.

This article is an observation of the consequences on all levels particularly on mental health and the young people being armed and sent into war like lambs to the slaughter. I was deeply moved by my friend's critical situation in Kyiv and felt compelled to write this piece on the tragic situation from varying perspectives. None of this helped my own mental health.

On a positive note, I was inspired to write again and wrote two true short stories, which I shall elaborate on further, and an article about CERN.

For those who know me well and my life stories, nothing particularly surprises them anymore… Despite being pretty much in the middle of nowhere for alone time, I managed to find myself embroiled in a bizarre relationship with an ex-legionnaire whose name translated is the 'Angel of Joy' - a story which blew everyone's mind including my own! I named the story, 'The Tortured Soul of the Angel of Joy' - a short story about the Spanish foreign legion, supernatural happenings, and a doomed romance.

I met him whilst on a mission to complete and upload my article on the war in Ukraine. Given I had no access to WIFI, I had managed to locate a small bar with internet facilities in the nearby small mountain village where I was staying. One coffee later, I was thrown out by the rather embittered ex-pat owners who made it clear it was not a Cybercafé. I had been warned about their unfriendliness but had chosen to my detriment to not enter into village gossip. Within minutes I found myself in a complete stranger's home, having overheard my angry outburst and dilemma, he very kindly offered the use of his internet to finish the article. It all occurred so quickly I hadn't yet had time to consider how the hell I ended up there nor where this sudden encounter could possibly lead us, but again, my writing took precedence.

I had asked the Universe to provide me with an ex-soldier for research purposes, for my writing I must hastily add. Having written and self-published two books and begun three more, I was attempting to work on articles and short stories to reignite my passion for the craft and to distract my rather fucked from life brain. Hence my getaway to a caravan in the middle of nowhere, accompanied by my laptop, notebooks, pens and some psychedelics to aid me on my journey of self-awareness.

As you have probably guessed, the romance did not end particularly well! Another life lesson.

In the meantime, I found myself falling in love with the area, the mountain walks, the proximity to the coast, clear starry skies and the thought of new beginnings and possibilities in a place with no personal history. My friend, who has lived in the area for almost three decades, offered me the opportunity to do up an old dilapidated caravan on his many hectares of land and create a home for myself there.

So, in May the project began. If you read my story in the first 'Memories' book you will know I have been preparing mentally and spiritually for years for 'The Great Reset', the shift, the global meltdown etc, and finally I was able to begin my true preparation for a place where I could become as self sufficient as possible and evolve into the mad wild mountain woman I have always been at heart.

When I first looked at the caravan, I almost ran a mile! Twenty years abandoned, full of junk, dirt and wildlife, it was not for the faint hearted! But I have vision and creativity and a multi-talented friend who has lived as a traveller since the 80's, plus the realisation that we could both help each other. Hence the real hard physical work began during the scorching Spanish summer. I write this in August taking a day out from the ongoing labour which includes clearing by hand an expanse of also abandoned land that was almost uninhabitable, with the occasional help of a couple of friends and one of my daughters…

The hard physical labour has been paramount in aiding with my depressive moments and seeing a dream slowly come alive. With barely any finance, we are carrying out the project with faith and the most basic of tools but proving what can be achieved with sheer tenacity. My friend, the owner of the land, has an old British ambulance, a bus, and a London taxi just to name a few of the curious vehicles parked up on the 40,000m^2 of terrain! We are brainstorming ways to create a living from the land with its many organic olive trees, and perhaps try crowdfunding. My dream is to be able to support ourselves from the land itself.

Whenever I feel overwhelmed and exhausted, I think back to my father in the 80's when we first came to Spain and his dream, to live on the land they acquired and build their home brick by brick over ten years at weekends, whilst working hard during the  week to support his family. He never gave up on his dream and he achieved it. I speak to him in spirit everyday and ask for wisdom and guidance. I know he is proud wherever he is…

Looks like it's going to be a very interesting few months - prices are going through the roof, all prepared and orchestrated of course, hence my rush to be as self sufficient as possible. It will be another huge distraction particularly as now the truths are being revealed about the jab amongst other things - they're definitely going to push people to the edge! So much going on!

*Links to my short stories can be found on the 'Memories' website **www.memoriesoflockdown.com** in writers comments.*

Jacob Melchizedek

There is no circumstance bigger than who you are.

As we move through life, we will be challenged. That's the beauty of life. It helps us to grow, to get in touch with ourselves and to be a part of the world around us rather than at the cause and effect of other people's choices.

When we acknowledge we are here for a purpose and we all have a unique piece of the greater puzzle, we know that life is happening for us, that we are supported and our authentic self-expression is important for assisting humanity, mother earth and all sentient beings. At this time more than ever, it's imperative we say yes to life. That we have a willingness to explore ways of living in harmony with our outer world by finding harmony within ourselves. This too isn't always easy. It takes courage.

It asks a lot of ourselves, and it can only be done with a true willingness to go beyond all the stories, beliefs and programmes we can hold so tight onto. There are ways to move through life with ease, grace and love. Even though we are still held in a very controlled societal environment, it is very possible to live the life you wish too. To live with others in harmony and thrive. When we truly know what holds true deep within our heart and we live from that place, life supports us.

It was early 2020 when I was guided to a Yoga Retreat Centre in the South Island of New Zealand. In March we went into lockdown. Twenty-two people from many places of the world living together on top of a mountain. It wasn't easy as everyone had their needs and wants. Somehow, we managed and had a lot of laughs along the way. I met a woman there and after a couple of months as friends, we became intimate. These kinds of situations can bring people together in that way, however, we actually had a very deep loving connection amidst all the chaos. Slowly more and more people left, needing to get home, to where they felt safe. Eventually it was Martine's turn, understandably she too was worried about what might happen if she stayed. We said our goodbyes in September 2020 as I dropped her off at the airport. We continued to be in contact over the next three months, which wasn't easy, not knowing what might happen and whether we would ever see each other again. So, we decided to have no contact for some months and get on with our own lives the best we could. After two months, Martine received a mystery email from me. It was an email with only a document of a book I was writing, which she had already read before. She thought that it was weird, however would reply anyway. Her reply came with a beautiful message inviting me to come and live with her in Spain. It was so beautiful to read, yet I was confused. I never sent her that email! Something was pulling us together and I took notice. We talked a few times and within a week or so I booked my ticket. We were to be reunited. I could fly to Spain unvaccinated on a three-month visitor visa. The day I arrived, the 24th February 2021, was the same day a year earlier Martine arrived at the Yoga Retreat Centre in NZ, where we met. It was amazing and we were so happy to be in each other's arms again. Then it got difficult. I couldn't get another visa and we ended up going to Holland to apply there, as Martine is Dutch. It took to the last days (four months) of the application for immigration to tell us it had been denied. I was given four weeks to leave Europe. We acted quickly and decided to appeal through a lawyer. Immigration said it would most likely take up to six months before we would hear from them. In the meantime, we had applied for NZ and Martine got a visa which was better than what was shown to be possible. Problem was, she had to be vaccinated to enter NZ. We continued on and did our best with the situation we had. It put a lot of strain on our relationship, me not being able to work and Martine having to do a lot of work with immigration around my visa. Also, we were finding it difficult to decide where to live.

In November 2021 my Dad in NZ was diagnosed with terminal cancer. This was hard to hear and it asked a lot of me in what I should do. Dad and Mum were saying, please live your life there, we are happy for you both, it is all ok. Martine and I talked about it, and I, more and more, came to a place that I wouldn't see my Dad again. I felt I was doing ok with this decision. As time went on and we talked with the lawyer, it was looking more likely our appeal would also be denied. There were several outside influences in our situation that made it difficult for us to create a home that supported us. We were being challenged and asked to really go within. I felt with everything that was happening that I needed to go home to NZ and be with my Dad and family. Martine and I talked a lot about us and our journey before I left.

I arrived in NZ on 15th March 2022 and stayed in MIQ (Managed

Isolation & Quarantine) for some days. It was easy for me to fly home without being vaccinated. However, it put pressure on me and my family as everyone was worried about me being a problem for Dad's health. When usually they would be open, all the doors to my family's homes were shut. So, I stayed with some friends while we figured this out. After about a week I borrowed a friend's campervan and went and saw Dad and Mum, finally. It was amazing to see them, and we were all happy to see each other. Surprisingly, not too emotional. The day went on and Mum asked me if I would stay for dinner? "I don't know, you tell me?" I asked. Mum showed the love for her child was more important than the rules around Covid. Dad too. I slept in the camper each night and spent a wonderful week or so with Mum and Dad. Dad was pretty good, and we talked a lot, he did need to rest often and was taking morphine twice a day and later more often.

I needed to get the campervan back to my friend as she needed it. It was really hard to leave. I went to the Yoga Retreat Centre for some days to recharge, feeling Dad was doing ok. Whilst there I got a message from spirit that Dad had gone downhill quickly. My sister messaged me that same day and said he was in the hospice, and she felt he wouldn't come home again. I quickly made my way back. The hospice had some strict rules with Covid, only two people at a time during visiting hours of 1pm to 4pm, and the unvaccinated (me) had to take an antigen test and wear a suit and gloves. That same morning, I arrived back, Dad had strongly requested all four of us kids were to be with him all at once. We managed to make this happen and with Mum there too, it was so beautiful. Dad was a lot more ill than before, however I could see this divine pure light shining out from him. It was something beyond being human and I will always remember this incredible gift.

The next day we went to see Dad during visiting hours, two

at a time. Before getting an antigen test and so on, I was told I couldn't go in. They said yesterday was a one-off and being unvaccinated I couldn't see my Dad, not until he was determined 'end of life'. Being the person I am, I was calm and asked some questions and the director of the hospice came and talked with me. He was apologetic and said those at the top made the rules and they couldn't do anything about it. He wished it was different as he found it hard as well. Many years earlier Dad's company made the windows and doors for the building, he did fundraising and donated to this very hospice. I accepted the decision and walked home.

We talked about it that night as a family. My oldest sister who is a nurse, felt this also was hard on Dad, so decided I would go the next day, sneak around the back with all the gear on and stand outside the sliding door so Dad could see me. I didn't need to enter the building or be close to anyone. This went well, even with one of the nurses seeing me there. They didn't say anything.

The next day Mum was having some difficulty watching her beloved husband of sixty-two years dying and wasn't sure about going up. Something happened with a phone call from a friend who had visited Dad earlier that made Mum decide to go up. I went with her and very quickly she got worried about me being there and said I needed to go. I got in the car and left. I had been doing well, however this hit me hard. Not being allowed to see my Dad, hurt. Seeing my Mum this way, hurt. I totally broke down.

I think it was two days later, Dad was determined 'end of life'. We could still only be there during visiting hours at the start. My sister, being a nurse was allowed to stay with Dad 24/7. This was a real blessing for us all. Dad hung in there for three days. I got to have some meaningful words with him, and I felt I had said everything I needed to. Sometimes it looked like he wanted to respond. We were all there with him when he took his last breath. It happened so peacefully. I am happy you are now at peace Dad. I love you.

It was about mid-April 2022 when we had a beautiful celebration for him and cheered his amazing life of giving so much. I stayed with Mum for a couple of weeks afterwards. Unfortunately, she got Covid after the funeral. That wasn't so nice for her, however it wasn't too full on, thankfully.

So, I am back home in New Zealand, broke and broken, not knowing when or if I will see Martine again. My Dad has passed, and I have no idea what to do with myself. I am happy to be in New Zealand. Familiarity is priceless. Martine and I know and trust in the process we will come together again if it's meant to be. These are the times to look deep within oneself.

As we know, this time in a pandemic, is full of the unknown and what I would like to share with you all is that the unknown is what's calling us home. Home to ourselves. To move beyond all the barriers and obstacles we have put up that keep us conforming, doing the same old thing, playing it safe and refusing to change. This pandemic has an aspect for us to question a lot about the world we live in. To really ask ourselves, does this feel true? Is this the only way we can live? How do I really feel about this and that? Can I do something to make a difference in the world? Hell yes. you can! You just have to believe in yourself through loving yourself and living from the heart, not the mind. Not by other people's choices and opinions. We have been taught to keep ourselves small. Not say too much or rock the boat. From little children, so much has been imprinted on our blueprint. Now, more than ever, is the time to put yourself before others. To come into the heart, be humble, kind and courageous, knowing you matter.

You are the most important person in your life and through this you will support others. Through loving yourself, you will love others. Whatever we do and be, we give others permission to do and be. This is how life works. Everything is energy. Everything has a frequency and is part of the collective. Know your vibe tribe can be found wherever you are. Find them and you will create wonderful things. Hold the vision of the world you wish to see as though it is here now because we are creating every moment with our thoughts, words and feelings. It's our responsibility to check in and see where we are creating from. Remember, your frequency is your currency. Use it well my friend.

The world is changing as we speak. All we have to do is choose to be part of the incredible New Earth that is unfolding. Yes, there will still be challenges and we will see things that aren't so nice. The thing is, we get to choose.

Choose to make a difference in our life for the better and that for our community.

Choose to know that you are amazing.

You are an amazing, incredible, loving, creative expression of the divine source creator. For that, I honour you. Thank you for being here. You are a gift and you are the one you have been waiting for... it's always been You. Be kind with yourself and open your heart. Watch the magic and be one with it all as it is happening.

Bless.

Jill from Noosa, Australia

When Rosanne first told me she would need to receive my story for her second book by the end of August, I started thinking about my last year and nothing in particular came to mind. I sort of thought… oh well it was pretty much the same as the year before - maybe I don't have much to add...

I'm not sure how far down I had buried my feelings or is it that I've learnt to live in the present because, actually, when I allowed myself to delve into the memory banks, it made me realise that this last year has certainly been an emotional roller-coaster and test of being true to myself.

Living in Australia has been interesting as we lived through a time of so many mixed messages. Mask wearing was compulsory in some states and not in others. Some states were under huge curfews and restrictions, locked down for literally months whilst others have gone about their lives relatively as before.

It was just too hard to keep up with the constantly changing rules and it became a very risky business to travel interstate for fear of not being allowed home. Stories of people stuck in border towns for months, living out of their cars - maybe they'd gone to see a relative or friend or even dared to have a little holiday away, then, within hours the rules would change and they weren't allowed back into their own home state. Some exemptions were given, but they weren't easy to obtain and how they were allocated is beyond comprehension.

During this time my sister's husband was diagnosed with a brain tumour and sadly has since passed away. One night after a really bad seizure he was taken into hospital by ambulance. We were allowed into the waiting room in the Emergency Department without masks or tests but were not allowed in to see him despite the fact we had been with him all evening. Luckily a really compassionate nurse allowed my sister to see him briefly to help alleviate his fears.

Another time I was in Emergency with a client and her family. We were asked to wait in a side room with two beds until a doctor could see us and while we waited several nurses and patients came in and out, all unmasked and untested. We waited for the doctors to complete their rounds and later that night my client was admitted.

My client was not in hospital for anything Covid related but as soon as she was admitted the same nurse who had been with us throughout the evening had to gown up, as did the orderly who took us in the lift. We were transferred into a special blocked off room and I went in through one door with my client and the hospital staff had to come in through another door, gowned and masked up, and they had to throw away everything after each entry. It seemed so ridiculous. I asked the nurse to help me understand how so many people could come and go, in and out of the waiting area, untested and unmasked then suddenly become a risk. The nurse quietly shared that it didn't make sense to her either as there was supposedly no coronavirus in Queensland at that time but she was just following the rules!

Eventually in early 2021 the vaccines started filtering through. Australia had a limited supply of vaccines in February, with them becoming more widely available in July, but with that were reports of complications and side effects and people really weren't sure what to do.A few believed the vaccines would stop the virus being so bad, others weren't keen but just went along with it because that's what they'd been advised and many were definitely against it, but too worried they would lose their job if they didn't have it. Some put it off until the very last moment and went in crying because they really didn't agree with it but didn't know how they would survive without having it, and then there were those who were never going to have it whatever that meant for their future.

Gradually towards the end of 2021 some of the borders started opening up and 'vaccine mandates' (some different again in each state) were being put into place. The dynamics of friendships were changing as there were so many differing opinions and so much pressure on people.

As a disability support worker for over twenty years, I was mandated to be vaccinated by December 15th, but as I personally knew of more people adversely affected by the vaccines than I did by Covid, I stood by my truth and retired just before the Queensland border opened on December 17th.

Mixed emotions and feelings. People were delighted that they would see family they hadn't seen for nearly two years, meet their new grandchildren, reunite with friends and partners, but even though only vaccinated people were allowed into the state, alongside the joy was the fear that this would open the floodgates to the big C entering Queensland.

Despite the fact that originally the vaccines were to protect us from the virus, we were now being told by the Health Minister that no one would escape it but "hopefully you won't get as sick".

So Christmas came and, as predicted, so did good old Covid. The normal Christmas gatherings were still messed up after two years as people started getting sick.

Some were quarantined, some isolated at home or at their holiday destinations, and queues were causing traffic jams with people trying to get tested. There were people with symptoms testing negative and people without symptoms testing positive. Businesses closed due to shortage of staff with people being sick or because they'd had one customer who was possibly contagious.

And then they ran out of tests! It was mayhem!

As 2022 has continued, so has the strangeness of our times. With so many people now working from home we have had a massive influx of the more wealthy southerners to Queensland. The prices of property sales and rentals has sky-rocketed forcing the locals out of the market and making so many people homeless. It has also created a staff shortage in so many trades, as ordinary folk can't afford to live here any more. Daily reporting of the Covid cases and deaths has now ceased, even though there are now more people sick with Covid, flu or respiratory illness than before the start of the pandemic.

People are now allowed in and out of the country without vaccinations, tests or quarantine rules, but many are still confused and some are caught up in the eternal doom of the mainstream media. I have seen families, friends, husbands and wives so divided and falling out over things that I never would have thought possible.People have been badly affected psychologically.

Where to from here...

Despite all of the above I still feel hopeful for the future. It is the Yin and Yang of life. I feel the big awakening is happening. There have been many freedom rallies, people of different cultures and beliefs vaccinated and unvaccinated all across the world together standing up for peoples rights and at last questioning their governments.

These times have allowed people to realise more and more what's important in their lives and have opened the eyes of so many as to how the world really is and how biased the media are.

We the people need to take our power back and life can be better. I am probably one of those people who has been labelled a conspiracy theorist, however, I see myself as a truth seeker - all I have done is follow my heart. I respect everyone's individual choice and all I ask is that they respect mine.

I believe as always 'Love Is The Answer'.

So until next year...

Sandy

During the Covid pandemic and lockdowns in 2020/21, I was writing what I called my 'lockdown lines' - many pages of observations and thoughts which I found therapeutic and somehow enjoyable. Writing is new to me. During the pandemic it became a way of observing and recording events, my moods and how I was coping. I am retired now and have time to do these things.

Now in September 2022, reading over my notes and reflecting on that period, I am still amazed at what happened. It was such a huge worldwide event, affecting everyone on this planet in so many different ways. I'm now walking around without a mask, hugging friends and family without many thoughts of catching the virus. I actually forget about it most of the time, even though I know many people who have had it recently, including my niece. After three weeks she is still lacking energy but having to continue with her self-employed work. It's so hard for her.

I remember being scared this virus could kill us. It stopped us all in our tracks. We weren't allowed out except for three reasons: shopping, medical need, and exercise. The Prime Minister caught the virus and ended up in hospital. Care homes were shut to visitors. Schools closed. The deaths mounted up worldwide.

Home schooling became the norm. For my dear grandchildren this was hard. They missed their friends so much. It was also extremely challenging for their parents. My grandson said to my daughter when they stopped their lessons for some lunch - "So you are my dinner lady now as well as my teacher!" "Yes" she answered, "I am, and I'm also the cleaner, the cook, the organiser and I have no classroom assistant. I barely have time for a tea break and have no staff room either!"

Exhausted partners worked hard too, doing essential jobs. My children shed tears on Zoom about how hard it was to juggle all this - their tears hard to witness, I longed to hug them. When one daughter caught Covid, I drove to her house and left a parcel of goodies on the doorstep, retreating to my car and waving at them looking out of their window. Wishing I could hug and reassure her, my motherly instincts severely curtailed. We Zoomed later sending each other virtual hugs.

Yes Zoom, that was all we had for many months of lockdown, speaking to friends and family, singing with the choir, yoga classes, a meditation group, a creative course, witnessing my life and family through a screen.

There were positives though. Walking everyday in the hills, usually on my own, loving the Somerset countryside. Seeing and really appreciating the beauty - raindrops on birch trees, sunsets, frost on grass, rhynes flowing with water, a kingfisher spotted at Ham Wall, a cuckoo singing up the hill. Nature didn't stop for this virus. I remember eating a piece of freshly made cake high up on the hill, admiring the wonderful views over the Somerset levels, relishing the peace. Roads quiet, no traffic sounds. Birds singing. No one going anywhere. It was glorious.

Supermarket deliveries were a new thing for me, and a chance for a few treats. I took some of my homemade cakes to a neighbour, leaving them on the doorstep. I'm aware how fortunate we were, not living in a flat in a city or even homeless, being able to walk in the countryside. I wondered whether this pandemic would change things? Wouldn't it be wonderful if everyone had a home to live in, essential workers got better wages, and fat cats regretted their greed? We clapped on our doorsteps every evening for the NHS workers, not forgetting the millions of other essential workers still keeping us going.

A few vivid dreams of Covid showed me I had a level of disturbance, of unease. I sometimes didn't know how to manage my uncomfortable feelings. This pandemic was a world drama. It was being shown on tv screens, we witnessed the sadness, loss and frustration of us all, the uncertainties and questions we wanted answers for. Everyone became tired of it, it went on much longer than expected. My daughter sent me an article about the possibility of post-traumatic growth rather than stress. I found that an interesting idea, of people growing in strength through their difficulties rather than being defeated. It was a time of extreme suffering but also I found some joy. A kind of full stop to the life I'd had and a time to discover new ideas and possibilities, like writing and drawing, spending time creating our new garden, and other projects. People were indeed creative, funny and inspiring. I loved hearing about a man who ran up and down the stairs for his exercise doing the equivalent number of steps to climbing

Everest! There was a woman on YouTube showing you how to cut your own fringe! Grayson Perry's Art Club on tv was a weekly highlight for me with people sending in their various creations.

I followed lockdown announcements seriously. I valued the research that the virologists were doing, especially when there were worrying announcements about new variants. I welcomed the vaccine rollout. I accepted the lockdown rules as we went along through the various changes even though they were deeply frustrating at times, with experts arguing about everything - full lockdown versus local lockdowns? The two metres apart rule or should it be more? Pubs open or shut? The rule of six? The value of face coverings or not, etc etc. I agreed with the idea that lockdowns were for the greater good. I could see that individual actions made a difference and were essential to reduce the spread of the virus. Older people were at greater risk if they caught Covid and mainly people were doing their best to limit the spread, showing compassion for others in incredible and caring ways. Maybe there were other ways to manage this virus but being in the more vulnerable category myself I was very careful to read expert scientific and medical advice and follow rules that made good sense to me.

Now reflecting on the pandemic and reading my notes I feel we have short memories. Why hasn't this changed our priorities? Made us appreciate workers and pay everyone a decent wage. Not start wars. Not run down the NHS by lack of funding. Covid disrupted us all in so many ways. It took away our lives as we knew them. It has been unsettling and hard. I would love to believe it has challenged us to adapt, to find new ways and appreciate what we have, but I'm not sure!

Hayley

September 2021 - August 2022

Life has improved since the end of the last book, it appears that many of us in the UK have returned to 'normal'. We've had no more lockdowns, mask wearing isn't a requirement in most places, no restrictions on entering shops or cafes, and we don't need QR codes. Travel has opened up for us all - jabbed and unjabbed - to most countries.

Some things are not improving however, and new or worse situations are developing with more fear in the media over war in Europe. It seems people only change their profile picture to that supporting Ukraine, or share information about their war but forget other countries currently also in the midst of one. It feels like because it's in the media and they are telling us about it daily, people then care, yet wars in the middle east or elsewhere are not so important that people share about it on social media, send relief aid, or accept a refugee, but for Ukraine they are happily doing it which feels biased, unjust and wrong.

We have had fuel shortages due to panic buying which probably wouldn't have happened if the media hadn't blown it up out of all proportion. Fuel prices rising, energy prices predicted to keep rising, and, if we believe what the news tells us, people will need to choose between buying food and keeping warm this winter. Are many of these things inevitable - a result of people sat at home on furlough for 6-12 months or more, due to the war, inflation or something else? How did anyone expect the country to survive after millions of people not working for months but being paid a high percentage or all of their wage… of course, we would expect to see inflation right around the corner. Or was it always part of a bigger agenda?

I have been lucky; I started a new job back in November 2022 and I feel very fortunate to have a better paid job and be doing something I enjoy. At the time I was unsure if it was safe to change jobs as so many people were losing their jobs and companies were finding themselves unable to keep staff on after lockdowns crippled the economy, but I knew mine would be safe.

In my new workplace we haven't had any restrictions since I started and although sometimes the staff were encouraged to wear masks, I was never under any pressure and had stated from the outset that I was exempt - it has not been a problem even though I am working around older people. On one occasion I was offered 'someone to talk to' - my response was accepted and since then I've had no further suggestions of a conversation.

When a colleague I worked closely with caught Covid, because I'm not jabbed I had to take 10 days off work to isolate despite feeling fine. I take great care of my health and keeping my immune system strong - I eat well, take supplements, holistic medicine and at the time my colleague became sick, I believed I was well, I didn't expect to be unwell, and I didn't catch Covid despite sharing a small unventilated office with that person.

I am still active in my local 'Stand in the Park' community, regularly attending our Sunday stand, though not quite as frequently as last year. There are not so many people attending on a weekly basis, which I think is due to the country seeming to have 'opened up' more, but we are still a large community.

We have created a Private Members Association called 'Camelot Connect' and we are connecting with more and more local groups in surrounding areas to share knowledge and support each other. We have around 50 or 60 paid members and growing, and we have regular meetings to discuss where the future is going and to prepare for what we think will come next.

We have also created a local 'People's Health Alliance' (PHA) Hub in our town. The PHA started in April this year as a national project, however, it is already growing globally. It has been formed in the UK to support people medically in many ways and prepare for the NHS to be so stretched they are unable to operate effectively. With the winter approaching, holistic practitioners and medical professionals are coming together and across the country the groups/Hubs are figuring out how to work effectively to give their community the help and support they need.

As I noticed a few people from my SITP group travelling abroad without having to have tests or proof of jabs, I decided to look at getting away. My friend and I went off to Europe for a week in the summer and despite the constant fear-mongering of cancellations at the airports and luggage going missing, we had the easiest airport experience; our flight was on time and our luggage didn't go missing!

We had no restrictions of any kind at the airport or when flying, and whilst we were away hardly a mask in sight and no rules to follow. It all felt like pre-2020 again. It was lovely to get away and not be led by fear in thinking something could go wrong or that it would be too difficult. I kept positive in my mind that I would have my holiday with no issues, and it all went without a hitch. I believe in positive thinking, imagining the best and not filling my mind with negativity like reading, watching and talking about things that are not positive as I feel you attract experiences to you. It certainly worked for me with my travel experience!

I think most of my friends around the world took the jab because they believed all the fear the media and doctors spoke of, and many probably still do.

One friend in Perth decided to not take the jab despite Australia making it hard to attend places and travel, and for many be able to work. She was allowed to fly to Bali recently because, although unjabbed, she said she had recently had Covid

Another friend in Australia was against having the jab but wanted to visit her family in Europe and was worried about not being able to fly, so eventually she gave in and had two jabs. She now realises the rules have changed and she could have flown without needing them.

I had a conversation with a lady, a stranger I met working in a shop during the summer who had had three jabs because she had a lot of fear around death due to losing a sibling at a young age. She had a relative who was terminally ill who had booked a holiday abroad so also felt she needed the jabs to go. She had convinced her children to also have the jabs despite them not wanting them and she had now realised the jabs were pointless as over the past months it has become known that they do not protect you from getting Covid or from passing it on. Also, by the time she travelled the jabs were no longer a requirement. They all caught Covid on their return from their holiday and were quite poorly, though the terminally ill lady less affected - the jabs hadn't helped.

She asked me about my views, and I gave her details of some videos to watch and suggested she grab a copy of 'The Light' newspaper so that she could read, see and hear the opinions of prominent figures, highly qualified doctors, virologists, scientists and pharmaceutical experts who have been speaking out from the start of Covid but been stifled due to censorship. These experts have risked their livelihoods and reputations by speaking out but because they went against the main narrative, they were unheard and even ridiculed. One of their messages was that they believed the jabs to be unsafe.

I love spontaneous conversations like this with open-minded people who engage in civilised discussion that are keen to share their views but also listen to new information, not shouting me down or dismissing what I have to say as a conspiracy theory. I wish more people behaved like this as I think there would be less division if there were more healthy conversations where people allow each other to speak and respect each other's views, and see that people have been subjected to programming.

I do understand that for many people it's hard to think that the government has not had our best interests at heart and that they've been lied to or to admit they were wrong to believe things, they'd rather stick with the same thoughts they've had right the way through.

To start unravelling the spin of the main narrative is huge, a lot of research, and it's much easier to just believe what they've been told than be branded crazy.

I object to being called a conspiracy theorist and told that my views are conspiracy theories. I have spent days, weeks and months researching, looking at statistics, reading articles and watching videos by people with long standing highly accredited careers.

I have been ridiculed and called crazy. It's very frustrating when it's clear to see that the doctors, politicians and scientists on the mainstream media are all saying exactly the same thing, and many are paid, have deals, or are getting funding for universities and studies they are doing, so they go along with it. It's nothing new - everyone knows that doctors receive kickbacks from pharmaceutical companies for pushing and promoting new drugs onto patients and this can be easily found online. What is new is the mainstream media not allowing a single debate since Covid began where groups of experts can discuss their different opinions.

Pfizer is the top pharmaceutical company with the highest paid lawsuits which anyone can read about online. Even the movie 'The Constant Gardener' is based on the true story of the pharmaceutical giant going to Nigeria in 1996 and giving unapproved drugs to children without prior consent, and how some died whilst others were left with life-changing injuries.

'Dying For Drugs' is an old Channel 4 documentary on YouTube showing how the pharmaceutical industry only cares about profit, and not people's health with pricing drugs out of reach for lower income families so people often die in poorer countries. There are some interesting real-life stories to watch.

I don't know what to think about how the rest of this year will turn out, or even the next 6 months.

Will things be as dire as the media predict?
Will there be more vax injuries and diseases on the rise?
Will more jabs be offered, and people keep taking them every few months?
Will children still be offered them despite the news that under 16's shouldn't receive them?
Will Doctors still prescribe drugs for depression that supposedly helps with a chemical imbalance despite a recent study disproving its effectiveness?
Will the economy collapse?
Will a cashless society be gradually introduced bringing with it a financial crisis?
Will more of our freedoms be taken away and our lives controlled, digital ID's and social credit systems?
I hope not.

I hope people wake up to the 'convenience' of things being pushed on us that are so called 'smart', quick and apparently will make our lives easier, to realise it is encroaching on our privacy, liberties and freedom to live life without constant surveillance.

I would like to see less division, fear and hate and less people taking pharmaceuticals.

I would like to see more solidarity, unions, love, joy and holistic health.

I would like to see people going back to natural health, seeking out homeopaths, naturopaths, herbalism, essential oils, nutrition, exercising, taking care of their emotional health and being accountable for their health on all levels, not seeking doctors to prescribe pills and medication for every ill, but realising that many diseases can be prevented and cured with holistic treatments that often have little or no side effects.

"If people empowered themselves with knowledge on health, nutrition and releasing emotions then the world would be full of much healthier and happier people living free of disease into old age."

*You can find details of the projects I am involved with on the 'Memories Of Lockdown' website in the writers section.

Rachael Martin

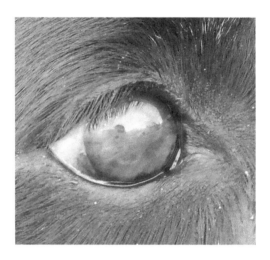

It was Saturday 18th April 2020, and I was on a day off thankfully - although my spirit was willing, my body and mind were already exhausted!

I was working as an Activities Co-ordinator in a nursing home and every Friday was 'Fun Friday' when I'd wear boppers on my head all day long regardless. On Easter Sunday I had kept the residents entertained by wearing bunny rabbit ears to the bemusement of one of the owners.

In the weeks before Easter, I had had the honour of running an 8 week 'Wellness Course' every Wednesday for our staff, teaching them Qi Gong techniques and meditations and I felt it benefited them and helped them cope with the situation we found ourselves in.

No matter how much we had prepared with endless daily meetings since February, how to put on PPE and how to cope in general, we didn't know what to expect. We were used to death, after all it was an end of life care centre, however nothing could have prepared us for the speed and number of residents that passed between the 16th of April and the 2nd of May 2020.

Every resident in a nursing home has co-morbidities/compromised immune systems, therefore, even the common flu can lead to pneumonia which in many cases results in death. The SARS CoV 2 virus did spread quickly once the first resident tested positive and it exacerbated any underlying conditions. We had 12 deaths in the first wave out of 62 residents who contracted the virus.

One of our lovely residents knew that due to his pre-existing health issues, he wouldn't survive if he got the virus and on the 16th April 2020, exacerbated by the SARS CoV 2 virus, he died. This was the start. I used to love our chats, and how he enjoyed his Guinness of a Friday. We were like family to him and all of the residents and vice versa.

I don't watch the news but according to management, the media were reporting people dropping dead in China and the virus was rampant in nursing homes, people dropping like flies etc., so you can only imagine the fear that was instilled in both residents who were compos mentis, family members and staff.

I was so grateful that my Mam who was in another nursing home, had dementia, as did a large percentage of our residents, so they had no comprehension of what was happening in the world. Oh and yeah, Mam's nursing home had gone into outbreak too - two or more people tested positive. A double whammy for me not knowing when I would get to see my own Mam. Thankfully only one death occurred in her nursing home in all of 2020!

Upon entering a nursing home, the sign that someone has passed over is the universal celtic Triskelion symbol - more noticeable now as we saw it more frequently. Each day our hearts would sink a little upon seeing this symbol.

The list of residents testing positive was updated daily, though we knew well before the list went up 'cos we could see it happening in front of our eyes.

From the first death onwards, all staff wore full PPE and had designated work zones. We used an empty resident's room to store clothes, and use the very santised toilet. Food was delivered to us directly from the kitchen. We had to wear masks at all times indoors and outdoors which I found ridiculous - I hated the masks, I felt suffocated.

Out of pure fear, management would shout at us to stay two metres apart from each other constantly, every day. Accusations that we were to blame. A lot of the staff were 'stressed out of their beans' or another way of saying it, 'they were up to high doe'.... more Irish sayings.

Endless temperature testing, and later endless PCR testing, and if you didn't have any of the typical symptoms at the time, you'd to go to work regardless of what else could be wrong with you! I became a temporary carer as staff consistently tested positive.

Carers living with other carers from other nursing homes had to move into a hotel. Health care workers were to spend as little time as possible with the resident doing hygiene but with maximum effect in order to minimise the spread of infection. This was very tough on our care staff as they battled with dementia residents who kicked, bit and screamed at the carers, and pulled off their masks.

We had fabulous weather and it was amazing to be able to spend time outside, to breathe in the fresh air. We walked outside around the nursing home with the residents who were mobile which was wonderful.

I'm grateful that I had my residents to hug, a risk I took and so glad I did. There were many times when my friends in the nursing home needed consoling, so we would nip into an unoccupied residents room (no CCTV) and hug and cry. I had my beautiful black Labrador, Kipu, which means happy in Tibetan, to hug each evening after work (RIP 06-Apr-2021).

It was a lonely time, and I didn't realise how lonely I was until I read my journal in order to write this article. I was connecting with close friends, Tricia, Michelle, Emer and Catherine, outside of work, mainly on social media while out on my walks. I'm grateful that I had the peace and quiet of my home and on my days off I'd lie out in the back garden under an umbrella listening to music, podcasts, spiritual teachers etc.

One funny moment when I was wheeling a trolley full of breakfast stuff and crashed into the door, spilling cornflakes everywhere, because my protective glasses had fogged up and I couldn't see - LOL.

I ensured I was taking high doses of Vitamin D3, C, magnesium, zinc and later quercetin and thankfully having my beliefs in the universe providing my love of the angels, energy and my act of service, I genuinely had no fear of going into an infected building every day.

I used certain energy techniques like zipping up my central and governing meridian and called upon angels to come with me through the door of the care centre each day. I must say I did 'up' the quantity, to a 100 million angels, sure why not, a lot are unemployed and were only waiting for a job. LOL.

It was an absolute honour to be with one beautiful soul as she started her transition back home. Some touching moments... singing "Somewhere Over The Rainbow" with this little angel who was on oxygen at this stage. That morning I told her I loved her so much and to go home to Holy God. We both told each other we loved each other - gosh I've tears as I write this now - not tears of sadness, it's human connection. It's an honour to be with someone at end of life, holding their hand, being present is a true gift to give anyone at any time in their lives. Her family, whom we knew well, did get to her in time to say their goodbyes. I felt it was important for my own healing, to clear out her room after her family had collected some memorabilia. In a strange way it helped me deal with my own Dad's passing over the previous year. It was touching to find her little slippers, this pulled at my heart strings, and funny when I found her stash of goodies! Strange to put all her belongings into bin bags to be incinerated and prepare the room for the disinfection that was now unfortunately common practice.

We all did our best to say goodbye to our lovely residents when they passed over, telling them we loved them. Watching the coroners quickly come in and place our little angels in a body bag, swiftly leaving the nursing home, was not common practice prior to this experience but unfortunately we got used to it too quickly over those couple of weeks. We did our utmost to form a guard of honour and waved our craters (term of endearment used in Ireland for older people) off to their next life.

Our priority was to keep our residents well fed, hydrated and loved. We experienced so much kindness from families who sent in goodies to us regularly, although I appreciated the delicious healthy sandwiches more than the choccies.

The moments of joy when our residents finished their quarantine and were back to their old tricks, slowly but surely. Seeing how the majority of the residents recovered to the best of their health, although the virus did knock it out of them for sure.

To see them eat heartily, engage in their activities again, singing, at this stage of course we'd still no live entertainment, so muggins here became DJ and we had a makeshift karaoke machine with microphones and disco ball lights. What a laugh... 'Stand By Your Man' - a given, sung by one of our residents who holds a special place in my heart.

Every nursing home interpreted the 'guidelines' differently and found ways for family to see their loved ones. I got comfort from the fact that families could start see their loved ones in our courtyard, initially from a distance and then from behind screens which really didn't make sense, in fact from the start I knew in my being that none of this made any sense.

Eventually by May 2021 families were allowed inside the building and could take their family member out for walks.

Going back to 2020, by late May I got to see my Mam in person, those two months seemed like years. She was wheeled out in a wheelchair and placed in front of me, while I was wedged between the main sliding doors of the nursing home, so not ideal!!

By July I was able to visit her in her room and it was then that she asked for a hug. My heart beamed with love. I also got to see my brother, sister-in-law and their kids and I got hugs - yeah! They could never have realised how important those hugs were to me.

In January 2021, almost immediately after the first Pfizer mRNA vaccine started being rolled out, some residents became ill and died in my nursing home. Mam's nursing home was hit badly.

My Mam was the only one out of 13 residents to survive. "Her soul contract."

I got a call early on 27th January 2021 to say that one of us should come in to be with Mam. I'd to phone my manager, who was amazing, because that meant I couldn't work for 14 days as I'd be in an infected building. This was another very hard day for me, and also my two brothers and their families. Mam was at end of life procedure, on morphine, shallow breathing. I stayed with her for hours, holding her hand with no feckin gloves by choice. My brothers cried when a carer told me I had to go as I was 'exposed' too long - for fuck sake. I've been exposed for months at this stage! I absolutely bawled my eyes out in the car after being with her. So the next day I stayed with her for the whole day.

I made sure she had an angel statue at her head, gave her Bio-energy therapy, called in the angels and to my lovely surprise the Director of Nursing was 'into angels' too. We sang Perry Como 'And I Love You So' with the carers, some who were bawling. A complete acceptance came over me. It's completely different when it's your own Mam, however I know the experience in my own nursing home really helped. My youngest brother managed to arrange within 24 hours to be home from France. My heart broke for my other brother who could not come up to the room to be with Mam. It wasn't Mam's time to pass. As soon as my younger brother arrived from France she turned her head towards him and possibly then decided to live. Wow it's not the first time we thought she was passing, but it certainly was the closest. She's just celebrated her 82nd birthday at the end of August, so there must be a reason she's hanging on.

2021-2022, and so it continued, whlie life went back to some sort of normality for others, we had outbreak after outbreak, rules shifting daily. We got through them - the residents were so resilient. We saw more of them than our own families. I stayed in the nursing home, until March 2022, although I had walked out in November 2021 and took health leave.

With a change of ownership in July 2021, things went from a heart-led management to a head-led management. Everything changed and for those of us who chose to opt out of taking the vaccine, we were risk assessed, which, in my view, was handled very badly. I wanted out of there.

The discrimination a small percentage of us experienced was unacceptable. We were listened to, but the situation was not resolved. We were understaffed and mentally, emotionally and physically exhausted. We didn't have the energy to pursue anything further legally... overwhelm and fatigue took over.

During the two years and four months that I worked in the nursing home, I learnt more about myself, my love and compassion for people just went through the roof. The influence I had on people, both staff and residents, by being truly myself. I learnt about self love especially, my pragmatic/can-do attitude, my triggers and my ability to adapt which I was aware of already. I learnt more about dementia and about the beauty in end of life. My belief is that you reincarnate unless you have dealt with your karma in this life. In June 2020 I walked 100km to raise funds for charity and in January 2021 I received a Mindfulness diploma plus a diploma for Mindfulness Based Stress Reduction, which I introduced to the residents. Lots was happening in my world.

It's hard to really understand what it's like unless you've worked in a nursing home or hospital but I hope I've given you an insight from my perspective of course, into my experience during 'The Retreat'.

So where am I now?

In January 2022 I set up a Power of 8 group; an initiative run by Lynne McTaggart. Every Tuesday I host a zoom meditation group whereby we set intentions for ourselves, for our families, for the collective.

In March 2022 I started working for an Irish owned wholefood company called Nourish. It's more in alignment with my beliefs.

Recently I've become involved with the PHA - the 'People's Health Alliance', and have set up the PHA Dublin Hub with a view to providing everyone with information on the choice of medical and/or complementary therapists, assistance and support for everyone.

My aim is to restart my Bio-Energy Life Coaching and Healing Practice with a view to incorporating all my knowledge into building a better future for myself.

I'm slowly re-starting my singing and salsa dancing hobbies face to face which is fantastic. I visit the nursing home where I worked from time to time and my ex-colleagues keep me updated regarding our lovely residents. I've been to a few wakes to say "fly with the angels".
    I'm just about to go visit my Mam and in a few weeks I will be flying back to my lovely Costa Blanca in Spain, and that's another story...

My story is dedicated to those who transitioned in 2020, 2021 and 2022, with gratitude to and for my close pals - you know who you are, my Mam Sheila, my deceased Dad Paul (Feb 2019) and my family. My trusty pal Kipu to whom I will be forever grateful. To Tricksie, who was my parents' dog, and is now so close to me especially since Kipu passed over, to the Archangels, my Guardian Angel, my Spirit Guides and to the Universe - God, Higher Self, Love.

"I love you to the Universe and beyond. Life is an adventure. All is well and so it is."

With love
Rach x
Bio-Energy therapist, Indian Head Massage, Qi Gong, Life Coach,
NLP practitioner, Mindfulness practitioner.

You can find me on the 'Memories of Lockdown' website in the writers section.

Kristin Kalnapenk, Estonia

To follow up on life in Estonia - it actually feels like the virus doesn't exist anymore. Nothing is closed or restricted, normal life is happening! I just get the virus itself from time to time.

Reading back my story in the 1st Memories book of how I had free time at home during lockdown sounds so relaxing, however, once I was back at school, I felt under pressure and unmotivated to continue my powered up lifestyle. My energy got drained and it was hard to keep up the meditation, sports and music besides the school work.

Having only 3 months of summer also makes it hard to keep up the energy - last winter was incredibly long, cold and dark. This last year of school - Autumn 2021/Summer 2022 - was pretty low energy for me but towards the end of the school year I was able to write some nice arrangements for my songs and took quite a leap in my composing skills.

This summer (2022) after I finished my Bachelor's Degree in Jazz music, was amazing. My life started to shine again - it was warm and sunny and I was feeling energised! The summer's in Estonia are so nourishing and the nature is so beautiful. My first idea was to continue with the Master's Degree in jazz music but at the last moment I decided to take a study leave.

Travelling to a warm country, taking time for myself, enjoying the beauty of nature and life sounds like the perfect thing to do. So, guess what? I'm packing my things and travelling to Australia with my partner and a group of friends!

We all got the working holiday visa and so we're off on an adventure with a one-way ticket without an exact plan for a return.

My aim for this year (2022) is to really level up my pole dance skills, finally release some music and write some new beautiful songs, and by 2024 I'd like to be ready for performances with a full band, pole dancing and aerial acrobatics.

That's a wrap up for now! I wish everyone great health and lots of energy!

With love,
Kristin.

Deborah Jane Sutton

'33 Quantum Truths that I learned in this Great Awakening'

1. Loving yourself is more important than you realise –
   Anita Moorjani was right – your life depends on it
2. Your level of consciousness is your salvation… and your
   new currency
3. Needing nothing, attracts everything
4. You are creating your reality through the vibrational
   frequency of your thoughts, beliefs, emotions and actions
5. Your 'reality' is actually a holographic projection of your
   energy and never has the frequency of your thoughts,
   beliefs, emotions and actions been more important to your
   future
6. Keeping them all positive is a priority
7. Understanding energy and raising your vibration is going to

become your main focus

8. You are the whole Universe in one human being

9. There is no one else

10. Others in your life are a reflection of a part of you. Sometimes a part of you that you like and sometimes a part of you that you don't

11. Due to #10 Forgiveness is always ultimately about forgiving yourself

12. Others cannot trigger you. They are merely reflecting back to you an emotion that already exists within you

13. The above emotion is asking to be acknowledged so it can transmute into love

14. Your animals really are your best friends

15. Random acts of kindness are the quickest and easiest way to shift your energy when you feel low

16. Being in nature is more important to your health than you realise

17. Faith carries you

18. Willingness to change is a pivotal point in your evolution

19. Television programs do just that – and it's not a good thing

20. If you are not excited, you are not on the right path

21. Your heart expands when something is right for you. It contracts when it isn't. Learn to tell the difference

22. Laughter is a necessity, not just a pleasure

23. People can only process information at the consciousness level that they are at

24. Although everyone can process the energy of Love on some level

25. Your children are more conscious than you realise

26. Heaven on Earth is not a place – it is a level of consciousness

27. Love is not an emotion – it is a state of Being

28. Dancing to your favourite music is better for your physical, emotional, mental and spiritual health than you realise

29. Doing what you love is a necessity not a luxury
30. You cannot solve a problem while still in the energy of it. Taking a few deep breaths will help you respond from a higher perspective
31. You are never alone
32. Your relationship with yourself is quite literally everything
33. When in an expanded state of consciousness, miracles occur

Please remember #17.
Faith is like an Inner Knowing – it carries you to miracles.
With Love and Blessings.
Deborah Jane Sutton
You can find Deborah Jane Sutton on YouTube, Facebook and at www.deborahjanesutton.com

When you understand that your future lies in your frequency, you realise that doing what you love is a necessity not a luxury

Barbara and Derek Ponsford

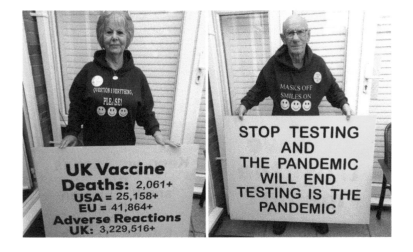

Derek and I met in 1963 and married in 1964. We have two daughters, two granddaughters and one great grandson. Our eldest daughter is Trudi and she lives in Australia with her husband Richard and our granddaughters, Ashleigh and Georgia.

Georgia is mummy to our beautiful baby great grandson, Myles. Kerry is our youngest daughter. She is a teacher and is at present living in the Philippines, teaching in a British International School in Manila.

I would like to start our story in 2015 as I feel that these events were preparation for what was to come in 2020 - it sets the scene. Kerry was teaching in Borneo then. We flew to spend three weeks with her and then three weeks in Australia. During our time in Borneo, my legs and arms were very badly bitten, I took advice and treatment from the local pharmacy with apparently no adverse side effects. When we arrived in Australia it was a very sad and hard time for us, as Trudi was very ill. She had been diagnosed with chronic Lyme disease, could hardly walk and was in constant pain. I'm pleased to say that now, with the help of a wonderful Naturopath she is very much better and is able to live a near normal life. It was a long few years for her though.

Moving forward to 2016 I suddenly started to experience a lot of medical issues, prior to this neither of us were ever ill. The first issue was I could hardly walk for nearly six weeks. The doctor couldn't find a proper diagnosis and this was followed by numerous other problems. I saw five different GP's during this time and I asked every one of them if the bites I'd had in Borneo could be anything to do with these sudden health issues. I was ignored.

Moving forward to August 2017, I had the most horrendous pain in the right side of my face and head, which was finally diagnosed as Ramsay Hunt Syndrome (Bell's Palsy and Shingles in my right ear). I was advised to see a Naturopath. This wonderful lady soon enabled me to get a proper diagnosis through blood tests, carried out in ArminLabs in Germany. I also had chronic Lyme disease caused by one of the bites I had suffered in Borneo, which all the doctors at my surgery had chosen to ignore. My doctor told me there was little the NHS could do to help me, so like my daughter in Australia, it was research and natural therapies that have helped me feel 95% better. I did have to have my right eye stitched back up at the local hospital because of the Bell's Palsy.

It was very difficult for Derek during this time, having his daughter and then his wife diagnosed with this horrible disease. It took it's toll on him, and for a few months he had to seek medical help, but he got better quite quickly, thank goodness.

I have told you of this difficult time because we did so much research and learnt so many things we weren't previously aware of, at times it was a real eye-opener.

I believe that during most of our married life we have always questioned everything and this is what we did at the beginning of 2020. We had just arrived back from Myanmar  in the January where we had spent four wonderful weeks with Kerry, who was teaching in Yangon at that time. The second part of our flight home was Bangkok to Heathrow, and I believe this was where we had our first encounter with Covid. A gentleman on the flight had the most horrendous cough, it was a cough like we had never heard before and he didn't stop the whole flight. The flight attendants were giving him many drinks but nothing helped, we felt so sorry for him because everyone was looking at him. I often wondered what happened to him.

Within a short time of arriving home, all we heard about was Covid - the TV wasn't talking about much else. All the mainstream news concentrated on Wuhan hospitals and people dying in the street. At first we watched it intently, though without any real fear, however we noticed that friends around us had become fearful.

One evening the news presenter announced that 'a doctor from a main hospital in Wuhan has been arrested for drawing attention to his colleagues that he was noticing something unusual with his patients'. He was put under duress to sign a letter saying he had been mistaken. This same story was repeated on other news broadcasts over a couple of days. Several weeks later it was announced that this same doctor had died of Covid in his mid thirties. This became our hmmmmmm moment… WHY to all of this???

In March 2020 the UK went into lockdown - we started doing our research and it didn't take long to see that things were not adding up. Why, when the WHO had downgraded the Coronavirus on 19th March, did Boris Johnson put us in lockdown on 23rd March? It made no sense and the more we researched, the more we realised nothing was making sense.

We reluctantly followed all the rules, but one day I received an eBook from one of my therapists. It had been written by a number of doctors telling 'it' from a different perspective and included 'The Great Barrington Declaration' - we read and signed it straight away. There was a lot to read and digest in this eBook but the thing that really bothered us was the warning of a forthcoming 'vaccine'. We immediately had a bad gut feeling.

By this time we were fed up with the 'briefings' and the 'next slide please' and it just seemed to be continuous fear mongering. We were only hearing about the amount of cases and deaths but no news on recoveries.

Christmas came and went and with it came the 'jab'. I refuse to call it a vaccine as it isn't. We had already decided that it wouldn't be for us, our decision was based on the fact that there was no safety data, no indemnity and it was still in trial until 2023. I had already checked with the Lyme disease association and they didn't advise it, and neither did any of my therapists.

When it was our turn to have the jab, we were continually hassled by our surgery and I ended up having a slightly heated discussion with a lady on the phone from the 'vaccination programme'. She was very forceful but had no idea about medical conditions and had never heard of Ramsay Hunt Syndrome. It made me very angry that this was allowed to happen.

By this time we were feeling very lonely, with our daughters overseas and all our friends rolling their sleeves up, we had no one to talk to. When we tried to voice our concerns to friends and even our family, we were accused of 'looking at too much Facebook' which we found very hurtful, considering how much research we had done and how many truths we had found.

We had almost reached rock bottom when one Sunday we heard about 'Stand In The Park - Yeovil'. We heard some very positive comments and on enquiring we were invited to join this gathering on the following Sunday.

It was the beginning of April 2021 and that first meeting changed our lives. We were welcomed and very soon made to feel part of a very special family. We went home that day very elated - we realised we were not alone, we weren't the odd ones out. There were thousands of us, not just in the UK but across the world. So 'Stand In The Park' became the highlight of our week, it was nice to have so many different age groups among us and each week more people would join us. The 1 hour meeting was turning into to 4 hours as we spent time getting to know each other.

In May we joined the first rally of our lives at 77 years old, it was in Bristol and we loved being a part of it. At the end of that month we joined a rally in London - it was on the May bank holiday Saturday and it was amazing. A group of us from SITP travelled up to London together. So many people, all there for the same reason and the energy was electrifying. No masks, no social distancing, everyone hugging, singing and dancing, and so many nurses, care workers, even doctors walking with us, it reaffirmed we were on the right side. We came home buzzing, but noticed there was no mention of it on the main news. We have attended four more rallies since then including one in Glastonbury.

From joining the 'Stand In The Park' we moved on to community meetings. We felt a bit like spare parts as we realised we didn't have the skills to offer that many people in the group had, so that is when our input became the Yellowboards. Derek and I purchased them ourselves as our contribution to the group and so it began. Our weekly 'Outreach' on the roadsides, outside supermarkets, hospitals, schools, colleges and most importantly vaccination centres.

As you can imagine we had very mixed responses, especially in the beginning. We were called words I cannot repeat, but as people began to realise 'all was not as it had first seemed' we started getting really positive feedback. People stopping their cars to thank us, many honking their horns. A young lad giving a £20 note to us to buy another board. Incidentally, this lad hugged us all and said we had changed his perspective on 'mature' people as, by seeing us on the roadside, he had realised we had not all just rolled our sleeves up and we had obviously done our homework! That same afternoon we had a very upsetting incident with a 14 year old girl, she thanked us for what we were doing and begged us to keep doing it - her mother had made her have the jab against her wishes and she was now feeling ill and depressed everyday. It was so upsetting to listen to her, it made us cry.

On another occasion a lady came and gave us four large boxes of chocolates to share between us to show her appreciation. The most memorable one for me was a 20 year old stopping his car and coming to speak to me. He came to say he was sorry for the times he had passed us and called us unrepeatable words. I asked him what had made him change his mind and he pointed to the board I was holding. It said 'Would you subject your small child to an experimental treatment?' He had gone home and researched.

He gave me a hug, said he was sorry and held the board himself for 5 minutes. That made my day!

If it changed one person's opinion or gave them the incentive to do their own research, it was worth standing in the wind and rain for.

As things are now changing rapidly, it is time to start changing the messages on the boards. One thing that is very important to us is to try and stop the 'jabbing' of the little children - it breaks my heart. Other messages for the board to make people think are - losing cash, digital currency, the nightmare of trying to see a doctor or dentist. It's never-ending.

And so it continues. It is now 2 years and 6 months since Boris said "3 weeks to flatten the curve." Every day we wake up and wonder what today will bring, sometimes it feels like we are living in a horror movie that will never end. I think both Derek and I feel worse now about things than we did a year ago. Derek is sad and I'm very, very angry. I know being angry is so bad for my health, but I can't figure out how to stop. The continual lies, tyranny and coercion from our government and governments across the world.

The ongoing continuous push to get people 'jabbed' while the amount of adverse reactions, including deaths, are being swept under the carpet. No one is allowed to speak out about it - it's terrifying.

The thing that we find hard to understand is how do so many intelligent people not join the dots? All the things that are happening right now: travel chaos, bus routes being discontinued, fuel prices, energy prices, not being able to see a doctor or dentist to name but a few.

I am currently having an ongoing battle with a local hospital over a small eye operation, they refused to operate because I refused to have a PCR test and they removed me from the waiting list. It has been ongoing for 7 months and has to go before the hospital board. I have sent them enough evidence for my reasons for refusing, including Boris admitting over 90% of PCR tests are false positives. I am not hopeful and the annoying part is, it is to put right what was done incorrectly the first time!

I decided to wait to finish our story to see if our daughter finally made it home from the Philippines after 3 years and 3 cancelled flights. I am pleased to say she did and many more happy memories were made. I believe she found it almost normal back here for 5 weeks, after the last couple of years in Manila where, for quite some time when they were allowed out, they had to wear a visor and a mask.

They still have to wear masks outside and all the little children have to wear masks all day at school. This really breaks my heart and I think is nothing short of child abuse. Hard to believe but she told us many hadn't been outside their homes for over 2 years!

So to conclude our story… I have lost several friendships of many years which I find very sad. I'm afraid the government have really succeeded with their divide and conquer plan as it has happened to so many families as well, which is tragic.

Have we gone down the right path? We think so. Recently at a 'Stand In The Park' event in another local town, I was called a stupid woman three times, the third time with expletives by a very angry man for not being vaccinated. I had to walk away, but not before I had replied to him. "Stupid for not having a genetic treatment with no safety data, no indemnity, and in trial until 2023. A treatment that people have had 4 shots of and still got Covid. I don't think so!"

Shelley

And along came Frank - more about him in a minute…

A year on - we are all happy and well which is the most important thing. Our children are both working hard and our daughter, Shanice, is planning her wedding for 2024 so that's really exciting and a wonderful family event to look forward to.

One of the main things that has changed over the last year is people's attitude towards us not having the jabs; there is no hostility from our friends any more which is nice - none of us really talk about it as if it's just old news. I think some people are waking up to the fact that these jabs are causing health issues and heart problems in particular.

A big personal change for us is that Neal's business, selling disinfectant, which was super-busy in 2020, has gone quiet for the moment - it seems no-one is buying disinfectant any more! Our turnover has gone back to how it was pre-Covid which has resulted in some financial stress causing us both to get extra work to make ends meet.

Personally we are grateful we have each other and we are all healthy; I find myself pretty tired of it all and tend to switch off most of the time - I think that's called self-preservation!

The world will never be what it was before all of this, and in some ways that's not a bad thing, but we feel the system has lied to us, that we have been lied to our whole lives and we don't know what to believe anymore.

Back to our Frank - he's just the biggest joy! He arrived aged 3 months, last November - we had been to see him once with his brothers and sisters and arranged to collect him 6 weeks later. He arrived and immediately turned our home upside down with all his antics. We were quickly reminded of all the hard work that comes with having a new puppy, but wow, he was and is worth every minute of it. Frank's just had his first birthday - he's a little ray of sunshine that shines brightly each and every day no matter what's going on in the world!

What a joy!

Mark Watson

From the island

Things began to change in 2021.

The cruise ships started trickling back to Patmos in the spring/ early summer. There weren't many of them and most were only half full. The tourists would emerge from the ships, hesitant at first, as if not sure if this was totally allowed. The islanders looked at them like long lost acquaintances – strange visitors from the outside world, but somehow familiar. Many from the ships wore masks in the square and window shopping the streets. On the tour buses up to the cave of the Apocalypse and the monastery of St John, they had to. Few Greeks did so, apart from those who went to services in the enclosed space of a church and a few, exceptionally paranoid, island holdouts like the Pilates teacher.

But something happened that summer which was totally unexpected. Normally, pre 2019, the number of visitors throughout the summer months was roughly 15,000. Double that number turned up in 2021. These were mostly independent travellers, many of those who swelled the numbers turning out to be club refugees from Mykonos. There the party season had started early and Covid had kicked in again. All fingers pointed guilt at the clubs. So they were told to shut down at midnight. Not so Patmos. Our clubs stayed open to 4, 5, 8, whenever the last people left a.m. - so the Mykonians took advantage of the new direct link between the islands and stayed out all night.

Travel in general for all of us only gradually got back to a relative normal. First you had to have a Covid vaccine to travel on ferries, but that was only minimally enforced and then seemingly abandoned. The default requirement became a negative Covid test, something the island provided for free for residents and for 10 euros for visitors. It being Greece, you were never quite sure what was actually going to be required; in the early days I saw someone at Piraeus being told to leave the ship because he didn't have a negative test certificate. But such occurrences were rare.

The island attitude to Covid itself changed that summer. The 3rd jab was offered but with the new less aggressive Omicron variant, many people, including myself, never took the offer up. After two doses of the Pfizer vaccine, for about 4 months afterwards my right arm suffered with a painful version of needle and pins. I later found out it wasn't the vaccine, but in the logic of my mind available to me at the time it was hard not to add 2 and 2 together, look suspiciously on what had been pumped into my left arm and come up with 4.

Throughout 2021 we heard of very few cases of Covid on the island. There were some but most people who got the Omicron variant recovered quickly. I heard of no long Covid symptoms of anyone on the island but some people who arrived, mainly French for some reason, were suffering from it. I heard of no deaths either, although interestingly this year I took a look at the cemetery and noticed an awful lot of people had died in 2021 – mainly older people. More than was normal. Was this evidence of excess deaths over the usual average annual number due to Covid? I don't know, but it did seem a little strange.

Autumn came, the visitors left. I continued with my online teaching; my wife kept up with her online work. We all swam into November, my daughter went out with her friends on the weekend evenings. There were rumours of the schools being closed down and things shifting back online. They weren't, indeed not one day was lost to the disease, which disappointed my daughter who was starting to think that 6 months of lounging around at home over the winter, or online home schooling as the government called it, was the norm.

2022 and it seems that we have slipped the tightest shackles of the disease. At least I feel that way. I've been careful in enclosed spaces, but a lot more lax than I thought I would be able to be so soon – the disease's hold on the imagination has been that strong. For me the less lethal variant has taken the sting out of the disease. There's a nagging feeling burping up into my consciousness every now and then that this might only be a temporary respite, and some mean in-your-face bully of a variant might muscle its way forward and drag us by the hair back into another lockdown phase. But, as the days go by and that doesn't happen, the small threads of confidence about surviving the disease, that it's not such a bad thing now, that it's truly on its way out are slowly meshing together, which feels good.

Or rather it should have done…

For it seemed like we were actually getting back to normal. The disease was disappearing over the horizon, people were coming back to the island, including my niece (though not her suitcase), the sun was shining, people were back enjoying themselves having carved out two weeks from their busy schedules to relax in the warm Mediterranean sun.

But then Russia made its land grab in Ukraine.

It had felt like the sun, poking out at last from behind the clouds after two years, was back and then this diseased dark moon had slipped over it and eclipsed its light. Not completely, but enough to cast more abnormal shadows over us all.

The last time I wrote I mentioned that living on a Greek island during the first days of Covid I felt privileged. This was mainly because we were cut off from the worst of what the rest of the world was going through. That started to go when all the visitors came last year and when the disease, if only mildly, reared its head for us all – we were more 'in it' than we had been. The feeling of privilege disappeared some more this year when the disease fell lower down the 'things that get talked about first' conversation list, but that was all right because if I didn't feel privileged it meant that things were returning to normal.

Then Russia attacked further north, but not that much farther, and that's spun things round for me almost 180 degrees because if things further north head south and nuclear weapons are used, with our north east winter winds, we are downstream of anything that happens on the Black Sea borders.

I felt privileged for two years. I still feel some of the old pre-Covid privilege living on a Greek island where the economy isn't suffering as badly as those in northern Europe (firewood for fuel is the new toilet paper in Germany a friend recently told me), our prices haven't jumped as much as those in the UK, the sun is out, we still swim and enjoy our outdoors café life.

That dark Russian moon is keeping normality at bay, the old normality that the pandemic put on hold, and that doesn't feel good. I have faith that the old normality will return. Indeed, it is still here: the purple-gold of the calm evening Aegean sea, the chilled glass of wine set out on the veranda table, the magenta bougainvillea, the first stars in the eastern sky.

It's just going to take a little longer to fully reappear than I thought it would.

Joe Hellyer-Gallagher

Written in August 2019 - a seemingly subconscious prediction of the future

Chemicals In Our Tears

When everybody's down,
you'll come around.
When everybody's near,
you'll be here.

Everybody has to go,
to keep the ship afloat.
No-one sees them disappear,
only chemicals in our tears.

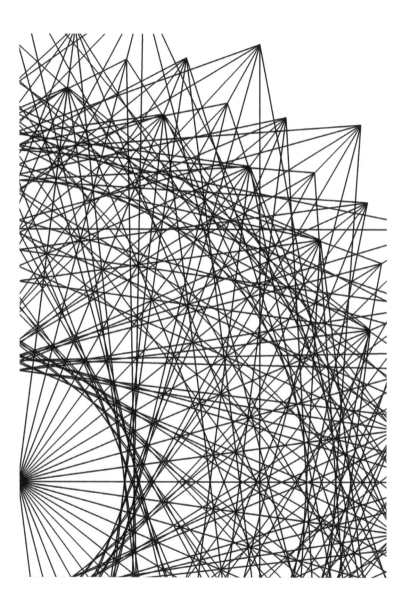

Conclusion

As we go into the last months of 2022 I feel we will see many more major changes in our world, in our way of life. I see more and more people disillusioned by the world they find themselves in and waking up to the fact that this is the moment for us to start creating the world we want to live in and thrive… not the one we find ourselves trying to survive in. The old systems don't work, they never worked.

Each morning I wake up brimming with excitement and in anticipation of what the day holds. I also pray each day for those who are living in fear, people who have no wish to carry on living in the circumstances they find themselves in. The world has changed and life will never be the same again and I find this realisation and the opportunities it brings very inspiring.

Day by day we are creating our new future, one that will benefit the majority, not the small minority. We are realising the power we have individually and collectively and I welcome the change for us all. We are stepping forward, following our hearts. 'Heart energy is the barometer of our future.'

To all my readers - if you have enjoyed reading this book, and maybe you have also read Book One… please look out for Book

Three which will be published in the autumn of 2023 concluding the trilogy.

Thank you to all the people who contacted me to write their stories in Book Two and sorry there wasn't room for you all. We will welcome new writers in Book Three - please contact me via the website.

You can find us on www.memoriesoflockdown.com

For those who have suffered through the Covid years, and I think everyone has now been touched by a little bit of heartbreak... I pray you can see hope for the future as I do.

"Sending love to you all and may 2023 bring everything we need to continue moving forward into our brighter future."

As we watch and see what happens as the world unfolds, allow the wave of change and embrace the knowing that WE are the change.

'The best way to predict the future is to create it'

'WE are the change'

Topics being discussed as we go to print at the end of October 2022:

Covid & Vaccines/Shots:
approved - experimental - athletes dropping down injured or dying - reports of serious side effects are very rare - vaccines rigorously trialled - infertility - follow the science - more deaths in 2021 than in 2020 - trust the WHO - children with heart conditions - tested & safe - sudden adult deaths unexplained - let fresh air in if meeting indoors - blood clots in all age groups - consider wearing a face covering in crowded, enclosed spaces - no debates on the BBC - marketing campaign urges people to get their vaccine before winter - censorship on social media - get your vaccine & boost your immunity - follow Dr Reiner Fuellmich - vaccine is best line of defence - the shot doesn't stop you from getting or spreading the virus - data showing a correlation with increased levels of cardiovascular problems - follow Dr Sam White - adverse reactions & deaths - safe & effective - booster for flu & covid available together - significant increase in heart attacks and other related illnesses since the COVID-19 vaccinations started to be distributed in 2021 - government will not open inquiry solely on vaccine safety - impact of boosters - potential risk - vaccine damage payment scheme is not fit for purpose.

UK Government chaos

Climate Change

Energy Crisis

Fuel Shortages

Food Shortages

Interest Rates

NHS

War

Inflation

Human Trafficking

Astrology

tension - clash between old world & new - centralisation & decentralisation - freedom & control - truth & clarity - cosmic & galactic energies - instability - evolution - intensity - earth upgrading - our cells upgrading - dizzying speed of ascension - turbulence around currency values - collapse of old - new financial system(s) waiting to be birthed - upset - upheaval - intense - emotional - trust - betrayal - many secrets coming to light - banking - hidden money - underhand money - shameless lies - control - jealousy - possessiveness - surges of energy - high frequency energy - taking us to a better place - create from love - focus on all that is good...

Solar eclipse 25 October - change ahead!

'When we look back on this time,
all that will really have mattered
is how we treated each other'

Lightning Source UK Ltd.
Milton Keynes UK
UKHW020801041222
413323UK00009B/109

9 781789 633528